CRITICAL DECISIONS IN FOLLOWING JESUS

Sermons For
Pentecost (Last Third)
Cycle A Gospel Texts

BY GEORGE S. JOHNSON

C.S.S. Publishing Co., Inc.
Lima, Ohio

CRITICAL DECISIONS IN FOLLOWING JESUS

BV
4300.5
J64
1992

Library of Congress Cataloging-in-Publication Data

Johnson, George S.
    Critical decisions in following Jesus : sermons for Pentecost (last third) cycle A Gospel texts / by George S. Johnson.
        p.   cm.
    ISBN 1-55673-427-1
    1. Pentecost season—Sermons. 2. Bible. N.T. Matthew—Sermons. 3. Bible. N.T. John VIII, 31-36—Sermons. 4. Lutheran Church—Sermons. 5. Sermons, American. I. Title.
BV4300.5J64   1992
252'.6—dc 20   92-7921
                                                                   CIP

9230 / ISBN 1-55673-427-1   PRINTED IN U.S.A.

In grateful appreciation to:

Vivian Elaine Johnson
Sonja Marie Johnson-Egertson
and
Joy Renee Wright

whose love, patience and encouragement
have enabled growth, fun and wholeness in my life

And in memory of:

Todd Russel Johnson

our son whose 15 years with us will be
remembered with delight and gratitude, as we
press on toward the call of God to follow Jesus.

In grateful dedication to

Vivian Elaine Johnson
Sonja Marie Johnson Garrison
and
Jon Alice Wright

whose love, patience and encouragement
have enabled growth in my appreciation of my

And Jesse Wright

Hope & Joy Johnson

our sons whose joy in Jesus Christ will be
remembered with delight and gratitude, as we
press on toward the call of God to follow Jesus.

Table Of Contents

C — Common (Proper)
L — Lutheran (Pentecost)
RC — Roman Catholic (Ordinary Time)

Acknowledgments

These sermons have been preached before the congregation at Our Savior's Lutheran Church in Circle Pines, Minnesota. I want to express my deep appreciation to them for their contribution to the spiritual formation of this pastor and to the formation of these sermons. Additional continuing education time provided by this congregation was used for research and writing.

I am indebted to works by Michael Crosby, Norman Gottwold, Jack Kingsbury, Walter Brueggemann and Jose Miranda, which helped me grapple with the scriptural texts. They are not, however, responsible for my interpretation and application. My theology and discipleship have also been more recently influenced by a number of liberation theologians.

The final stage of putting this book together was done at ARC Retreat Center near Cambridge, Minnesota. Their kind hospitality provided a wonderful atmosphere in which to work. A special thanks to Carol Morgen for putting all these words into the computer, my wife Vivian for her helpful suggestions, and to Lowell Erdahl, friend and Bishop, who encouraged me to take on this project.

Acknowledgments

Foreword

This is a remarkable collection of sermons that has been prepared by a remarkable person. Few of us have had the unusual combination of life experiences that has been part of George Johnson's history. Experiences that often stand in contrast and sometimes intense conflict with each other have come together in his life. This diversity finds expression within this unusual and possibly unique collection of sermons.

George Johnson comes from an evangelical tradition and began his serious study of scripture at the Lutheran Bible Institute. All of these sermons reflect honest wrestling with biblical texts and a couple of them will especially warm the hearts of the teachers he had at LBI. George preaches with conviction and is not ashamed to call for repentance and conversion.

George Johnson is also acquainted first hand with the suffering and oppression of millions on this troubled planet. For seven years he was director of the American Lutheran Church's World Hunger program and traveled extensively in Third World countries. From that experience George has developed a commitment to justice and peace that matches his commitment to personal conversion. If some of these sermons sound like they might have been preached by Billy Graham, others sound like those coming from Bill Sloan Coffin or other prophets of social justice.

In bringing together these themes of evangelism and social justice George Johnson is to be highly commended. We need clear personal gospel proclamation that evokes personal faith and discipleship. We also need clear prophetic preaching that exposes the injustice of corporate, as well as personal evil that is part of life in our world.

This preaching is life-situational as well as textual. These are not religious lectures. They are sermons addressed to specific people wrestling with the current issues in life. The language is personal and the illustrations frequent and insightful. There is nothing simplistic or superficial about these sermons, but there is an easily understandable clarity in their expression.

Johnson's sermons are evangelistic and prophetic, personal and social, Biblical and life-situational. If they inspire others to follow the model of his example, they will do a significant service for our church and our world.

Lowell O. Erdahl
Bishop, St. Paul Area Synod
Evangelical Lutheran Church in America

Introduction

Speech is critical to human development and interaction. Preaching is one form of speech, and as such is vital to the life of the church. It is part of the mystery of our faith that God uses preaching to call, gather and enlighten the whole Christian Church. What follows in these pages is a series of sermons that attempt to give speech to the story found in the Bible.

I have serious questions about the need for another book of sermons. Reading someone else's sermons is not the greatest delight of any pastor. Sermons are meant to be preached, not read. Something is missing when the people who listen are not present and the presence and personality of the preacher is not visible.

Sometimes, however, even the written sermon can serve to strengthen another person's preaching. Ideas spark ideas. One person's journey into a text can open up new vistas for the one looking for a way to gain insight and imagination for proclamation. The sermons in this book were written to be delivered before a particular congregation, not for a book of sermons. Please keep this in mind.

Preachers never preach alone. There are no solo flights. We always enter the pulpit having been influenced by the sermons of others. A new and fresh sermon is indebted to many sermons that have shaped the life and theology of the author. Add to this the realization that the sermon heard is received by someone who has most likely heard many sermons. The sermon being preached is interpreted in light of previous sermons preached and listened to. While I take full responsibility for what is said in these sermons, I also am humbled in the awareness that preaching belongs to the church, not to any individual. You will hear in these sermons the voices of many who have shaped my thinking and interpretation.

11

Dr. David Preus, the former presiding Lutheran Bishop, told a convention attended by pastors that one of the greatest sins of the church today is conducting Sunday worship that is dull and boring. I think he was right. After hearing this, I have given new energy to sermon preparation. Though the sermon is not the only reason people of faith gather for worship, if the sermon is dull and boring, it is hard to make up for it with meaningful liturgy, music and prayers. Preaching is still central to the life of the church.

Walter Brueggemann states in his book, *Finally Comes the Poet*, that preaching is demanding, daring and dangerous. The more I preach, the more I have become aware of this. Good preaching requires continued and careful study of the text and the historical context of the situation in which one speaks. When the risk of preaching has been avoided we have, as Brueggemann suggests, a gospel that has become "truth greatly reduced, a truth that has been flattened, trivialized and rendered inane." Good preaching is dangerous in the sense that it makes claims that are contradictory to many social norms and accepted values. It is subversive because it calls for decisive actions that would bring about change in the present systems of exploitation and death. It disturbs those who benefit from the present arrangement of things.

I like to preach. I even like sermon preparation. Besides the ego building that happens in any speech giving, I enjoy preaching because I know that I am participating in a very critical moment in the life of the church. Exciting things happen through preaching. Life-changing decisions are made. Foundations are shaken and shaped. The Holy Spirit is acting to bring about healing and harmony. There is always that surprise element. One never knows just what will happen or how the sermon will be used by God. I try to preach with the confidence that somewhere, somehow, God is converting, calling, comforting and challenging. It is a kairos event, a time of opportunity filled with potential.

Preaching for me is a *dramatic moment* when the story that is old and familiar is told once again to a new situation with fresh energy. It is a *healing moment* when pain is embraced and the balm in Gilead restores to wholeness what is hurting and separated. Preaching is an *artistic moment* when speech is given life and meaning through carefully chosen words, images and stories. The combination of a text, a preacher, an audience and a situation in history results in a tapestry of communication. It is a *critical moment* when decisions are made and God's yes invites a yes from the listener, a yes that also involves a no, a letting go as well as a holding on. The preacher never knows who might be hearing a sermon for the last time. As a pastor, I feel privileged to be one of the participants in this *powerful moment* in the life of God's people. The prayer I enter the pulpit with is, "May the word of God speed on and triumph among us."

Most of the texts in this series come from Matthew's gospel. Matthew has a unique contribution to make to our understanding of Jesus because of who Matthew was. Sermons based on Matthew texts will be influenced by his understanding of the kingdom of God, discipleship, Jewish influence, and the expectations of God in the lives of Jesus' followers. Matthew, for example, addresses the house churches of his day where the economy of the household was closely tied to discipleship. Members of the house churches were apparently more wealthy than poor and so the dangers of wealth are confronted. The will of God and what it means to be righteous (just) are themes throughout the book reaching a climax in the Great Judgment scene in Matthew 25.

The series of texts for the last third of Pentecost carry some common themes. The events and teachings of Jesus are from the end of his life on earth. They contain a note of urgency with an element of "wake up or else" in many of the passages. There is an eschaton, and in view of that future happening, Matthew desires to shape the life of discipleship in the present. Some of the themes I see reappearing in these texts are:

13

The Judgment Of God

It's almost overwhelming at times. Tenants of the vineyard are put to a miserable death. The kingdom is taken away from them. Those who reject the invitation to the marriage banquet are destroyed. The king was enraged. A guest with no wedding garment is cast into outer darkness. The exalted are humbled. The five bridesmaids without are shut out. The consequence of not investing the one talent is weeping and gnashing of teeth. And finally, the goats who did not feed the hungry are cast into eternal punishment prepared for the devil and his angels. Put all that together and you have one heavy load. God does not take rejection lightly.

One cannot preach from these texts without dealing with the judgment of God. To do so would be to make the gospel a "truth greatly reduced." We miss the point of how hurt God really is over the pain and injustices in society when we sidestep the judgment theme. There are consequences to the way we live our lives. We are accountable to God. There will be a dividing line.

We cannot find in these texts a convenient shield from God's judgment by calling upon God's unmerited love. It is *love* that calls forth judgment. God is not indifferent to our actions. The theme of judgment means that God notices how society functions and how we relate to those in need. It really matters to God. Judgment warnings are a sign of hope because it calls for repentance and renewed alertness. The judgment speeches create within the church a new hunger for the meaning of justice and righteousness talked about in the beatitudes. Understanding the judgment of God enables the follower of Jesus to make good decisions.

Crisis Of Decision

Jack Kingsbury in his *Proclamation Commentary on Matthew* demonstrates how many of the Matthew passages "make it clear that encounter with the earthly Jesus placed a person in a crisis of decision.'' Choices needed to be made. An encounter with the kingdom preached by Jesus required a person to decide. Jesus himself had to make some critical decisions. So do we.

As the fundamental criteria of true discipleship are spelled out by Matthew, it is up to the listener to decide whether to follow. There are two gates to enter. One is narrow and one is wide. One must choose. Our choices have consequences. That's what makes it a crisis of decision. It really matters what we decide.

There is also a sense of urgency to our decision. To put off one's decision is to become like the bridesmaids who found themselves caught short of oil. It was too late to decide once the bridegroom came. Even their last minute plea did not help overcome their lack of decisive action.

Preaching, I believe, needs to call for a response from the listener. To be faithful in our proclamation, the preacher is expected to herald the good news in such a way that the person addressed is encouraged to make a decision of some sort. This kind of preaching does not take away the giftedness of our salvation, nor does it reduce the gospel to some kind of human endeavor. Instead, preaching that evokes a decision leads one to meaningful discipleship, a life committed to justice and righteousness. There is a sense in which the church today is at a kairos moment, a special time calling for decisive action before the opportunity is lost. Each time we step into the pulpit, it is a kairos moment.

Following Jesus

Matthew portrays Jesus as one who invites people to follow him; not just believe in him, but follow him. The proclamation of the kingdom is an urgent call to take up one's cross *and follow*. From that stance, the gospel of Matthew is written to show what it means to follow, what is expected of those

15

who accept the invitation to follow. The Sermon on the Mount sets forth what following Jesus involves, as do the parables and events in the life of Jesus.

The life of following Jesus consists of a "greater righteousness" (justice) than that of the scribes and the Pharisees (Matthew 5:20). Followers are to seek first the kingdom of God's righteousness (justice). Michael Crosby in *House of Disciples; Church, Economics and Justice in Matthew,* helps us understand Matthew's concern for justice in the life of following. Justice is the bottom line that God looks at in making judgments about who is following. Because the church for Matthew is a household of followers and economy is the management of the household, Crosby sees an intimate connection between economics, church and justice in following Jesus.

Like the other gospels, Matthew demonstrates that love is a hallmark of following. Love for God and love for neighbor are the sum and substance of all the commandments. Following Jesus is learning how to do the loving thing in our relationships both individually and as a household.

Preaching that articulates the gospel's invitation will use terms like "following Jesus" frequently. This avoids the tendency to think of Christianity as being something intellectual, a mere acceptance of certain beliefs. The church that Matthew envisions is not only a household of believers, but a household of followers. The wise people are those who build on the rock which means doing the will of God as followers, not just believing that God loves you and Jesus died for you.

Justice And Righteousness

Anyone preaching from Matthew must become familiar with the meaning of *dikaiosyne* which most versions translate as righteousness. A better translation might be justice. As the meaning of dikaiosyne unfolds through the book, it is seen as a fulfillment of the Torah and Old Testament covenant terms "mishpat and zedekah" which are translated justice and righteousness. Matthew seems to operate under the assumption that the readers are familiar with these covenant concepts. Most of our listeners are not.

Dikaiosyne (justice) for Matthew has both the meaning of God's saving presence and the right ordering in human relationships and resources that bring about the will of God. Members of the household are to witness to the saving acts of God's justice by their own acts of justice in society. The kingdom Matthew talks about is a kingdom where justice is done. The blessed in the beatitudes are those who hunger and thirst for this justice. Disciples need to know what the content of this concept includes. Preaching needs to clarify this.

Jose Miranda in his book *Marx and the Bible* has a helpful discourse on the biblical use and meaning of justice (pp. 44-160). With skillful exegesis he shows that the essence of God is justice, and how love of neighbor and justice are inseparable. Michael Crosby's reference to justice as the right ordering of relationships and resources helps one to see the practical implications of the concept. Mishpat and zedekah cannot be promoted in the abstract but only in the human situation where injustice occurs. When Matthew reminds followers of Jesus to seek the kingdom and God's justice (Matthew 6:33), it brings out the meaning of the moral implications for our lives in the here and now.

The just person has compassion and shares resources. Justice means being in solidarity with people who have been exploited, neglected and oppressed. Justice is discerning what belongs to whom and returning it, if necessary. A special focus for God's justice is the poor, the forgotten ones in society.

An example of what justice means is found in Psalm 82 where the expulsion of divine beings from God's council is described. They were kicked out because they did not do justice, they did not rescue the poor and needy. The prayer for the king in messianic Psalm 72 centers around the king's task of defending the poor of the people. Jesus came to fulfill this messianic role, to preach good news to the poor. The Bible continually pictures God as one who sides with the poor and oppressed.

17

At the heart of Matthew's gospel is not God's gift of forgiveness, but the kingdom of God as announced and lived out in the life of Jesus. Matthew's understanding of the kingdom ethic calls for a response to the needs of people that are both physical and spiritual. It involves a reordering of economics in the household of faith as well as the household of society so that justice is done. To be in solidarity with the poor and oppressed includes not only sharing bread with them, but also being against that which oppresses them. To know and understand this is what makes preaching a demanding enterprise. Pope John Paul II, during his visit to Canada in 1984, said it well:

> *"The needs of the poor take priority over the needs of the rich; the rights of the workers over the maximization of profits; the preservation of the environment over uncontrolled industrial expansion; production to meet social needs over production for military purposes."*

In Summary

The reader will find these themes surfacing frequently in the sermons that follow. For me they are operating assumptions that are present in all the Pentecost texts. They help us understand who Jesus is and what he stands for. It is the task of preaching to present this Jesus to the weekly audience. Such interpretation is demanding, daring and dangerous.

The task is formidable because the ideological forces that are at work in our society are often opposed to these kingdom goals. These forces are deeply embedded in the thinking of those invited to follow Jesus. Preaching should always be done with an awareness of the idolatry that is present in society. We preach with the confidence that God is calling people today to radical discipleship. We proclaim the gospel with the authority and power, believing that God is with us to the close of the age.

What's The Bottom Line?

What are your thoughts when you first wake up in the morning? What am I going to wear today? Is the bathroom free? What's the weather like? Can I stay in bed just a little bit longer?

I am waking up earlier now that I'm on the other side of 50, the second side of life. My thoughts early in the morning are usually around the day's appointments. Let's see, Lois needs that article by 9. I could go to the hospital over the lunch hour. Confirmation is today. What meeting do I have tonight? Will Viv and I have dinner together? So goes my thinking early in the morning.

Seldom do I think about what life is all about or why am I doing all this, why am I here? Those deeper questions about the meaning of life come on rare occasions — usually when I have time to think or meditate, when I read a good book or take time to get away from my daily routine. Once in a great while when I get extremely frustrated, when everything seems to go awry, or no one seems to appreciate my efforts, I will sit back and ask myself, "Why am I doing this? What is it for?"

We all need to stop and ask the deeper questions once in a while, as individuals and as a church. Why am I here — why are we doing this — what's the bottom line?

19

In our text from Matthew we are encouraged to ask the question, when all is said and done, what's the bottom line. What is our ultimate purpose for living? What is God looking for? If we believe there is a God, what are God's expectations.

Yes, I am to believe in God — trust the promise, follow Jesus. But why? Yes, we are to obey the 10 commandments. But why? Yes, we are to pray, ask for forgiveness, love our neighbor. But why? Yes, we are called into community and we are to worship together, praise God together, be present to one another. But why? What's the bottom line, really? What is God looking for? What is the harvest that God, the landowner, is expecting to receive when the season is over?

The text in Matthew is a parable about a vineyard. The owner sends servants to collect the harvest from the tenants. But the servants are treated shamefully. Instead of fruit — beautiful and tasty grapes in abundance — there is violence and death. To help us understand this parable, it is good to be familiar with the first lesson for today from Isaiah 5, where we have another story of a vineyard.

Remember the setting in Isaiah. God chose a people, the Jews, and he said to them, "I want to bless you, and by you, through you, I want to bless the whole world. You are the instrument that I will use to restore — bring back into harmony what I have created in beauty and splendor." So God established a covenant with this special nation called the Hebrews. I will give you this and this and this. I will do this and this and this. So that you will be a blessing to the whole world, I will provide you with everything you will need. These are my expectations.

Every once in a while God has a review with Isreal to see how things are going. Are they still in focus? Do they understand what is expected, what the bottom line is? Isaiah 5 is one of those reviews. The audience listening to Jesus tell this parable was very familiar with the song of the vineyard in Isaiah 5. Here's how it starts.

"Let me sing for my beloved a love song." Doesn't that sound romantic? It makes you want to read on. God's love is set to music, a love song. It is because of God's love that we have this story. Remember this setting because as we move into the story, we may wonder where love fits in.

The lover, who is God, has planted a vineyard. Stories from nature that contain deep truths abound in the scriptures. This is one of the most compelling. To have the best harvest of grapes, to make sure the grapes are good, sweet, tasty and high quality, the lover who owns the vineyard pulls out all the stops. Notice what is done for the vineyard.

A very fertile hill is chosen, a hill with potential, a hill that has promise, a hill with rich soil. It is cultivated. It is cleared of stones. When I lived on a farm in western Minnesota I remember how every year we had to clear stones away. They kept coming up out of the soil. Those of you who know farming can appreciate what it means that the vineyard was cleared of stones.

The owner now goes to the nursery and looks for the best, choicest vines to plant. He doesn't care how much it will cost. He wants the best. Every effort is made to make sure that the grapes are top quality, sweet juicy grapes.

Fertile soil, good cultivation, stones cleared out, choice vines planted. How can you go wrong? But more is done to ensure the desired results. He builds a watch tower so all dangers can be detected ahead of time. There is protection from enemies. A wine vat is built close by to get ready for the harvest. The owner does everything to make a good harvest possible.

Now the author of the story brings us into the picture. "What did I leave out," God asks. Judge, I pray you — you be the judge — what more should I have done? Did I forget anything? When I looked for it to yield grapes, why did it yield wild grapes?

The term wild grapes in the Hebrew language means very bitter grapes, grapes that rot your teeth, grapes that make you want to vomit, just terrible tasting grapes, repulsive — not just mediocre or inferior, but bitter. Not acceptable at all. Of no value to anyone.

What happened? What did I do wrong, God asks. Why did this happen? I worked so hard and I looked forward to those sweet tasting grapes. Why did the vineyard produce wild grapes?

The key to the whole story is found in verse 7 of Isaiah 5. Here is the application. The story of the vineyard is pretty clear. The application is very revealing. It is heavy. The vineyard is the house of Israel. The men and women of Judah are God's pleasant plantings. In other words, the chosen people of God are the recipients of all the good things God did in order to produce the fruit looked for. They were blessed to be a blessing.

What was God looking for from Israel? What was the bottom line? "God looked for justice, but behold, bloodshed. Righteousness, but behold, a cry." In the Matthew parable we have the same image of a vineyard. The owner is looking for a harvest, but instead, violence and bloodshed. The two stories are linked.

What God is looking for is justice and righteousness. The Hebrew words are mishpat and zedekah. They are constantly used together in the First Testament. In fact, these two concepts permeate all of scripture. They are what the kingdom of God is about. The meaning is there even when the words are not used. Everyone who is serious about the Bible must be very familiar with the Hebrew terms mishpat and zedekah. Without an understanding of these two concepts, you will never understand God nor God's expectations, not the God of the Bible.

Parents should be careful to send their children to a Sunday school or confirmation program that teaches their children about mishpat and zedekah. Without a clear understanding of these concepts, they will never know what their baptism signifies, what the bottom line is, what God expects from us, what God wants to happen in the world. They may know about all the things God has done for us. God dug it, cleared it of stones, planted a choice vine. Yes, God so loved the world that God gave his a Son. Yes, God gave us the scriptures, the sacraments, the Holy Spirit, the church.

But what good does it all do if the harvest produces wild grapes? What good is knowing all that God has done and promises, if we don't know what mishpat and zedekah (justice and righteousness) are. Make sure your children know what God is looking for — what the bottom line is. It is mishpat and zedekah. Did you notice what the text says will happen when these are not present? The owner said, "The kingdom will be taken away from you and given to a people producing the fruits of the kingdom."

What kind of grapes is God looking for? What do we know about these words mishpat and zedekah? What do they mean? One simple definition is that justice and righteousness means the right ordering of relationships and resources. God made this world to work. It works only in the right ordering of relationships and resources, when people learn to cooperate instead of compete, love instead of dominate.

It involves our relationship to God. It involves our relationship to the earth. It involves our relationship to one another. It involves our relationship to ourselves.

When any of these relationships and resources are broken, weakened, distorted, neglected, that's when injustice occurs. The world doesn't work. God calls us and redeems us, so that justice and righteousness might restore those relationships and resources. The kingdom is about healing and making whole that which has been broken. It is about mishpat and zedekah.

When mishpat and zedekah are absent God brings judgment. When there is no harvest of good grapes the kingdom is taken away and given to someone else. God's love abounds so that justice may happen, so that the world may work for everyone, not just a few.

In some religious circles today you might get the impression that the bottom line is emotional stability, having a good feeling inside of us, being at peace with God, knowing our sins are forgiven. Is that the end? No. The inner peace we experience is God's gift so that mishpat and zedekah can happen. Some religious groups stress correct doctrinal statements. Having right beliefs — pure teaching, correct liturgical forms — good preaching from God's Word is stressed as central. All this is great, but that's not the bottom line. Justice is.

Is God saying to our church today, what more was there for me to do for you that I didn't do? I gave you a good beginning. By grace you have been saved. I gave you reformers, prophets, the catechism, great music. I gave you sound teachings and a strong emphasis on Bible study. I looked for mishpat and zedekah, justice and righteousness. I expected to find a people who worked for the right ordering of relationships and resources so that all creation might be blessed.

We have a wonderful heritage of music. I love to hear our church college choirs. They are able to lift the soul in adoration and praise. We have a music director who can make singing come alive in our church. Our worship team has introduced us to an alternative style of worship. Many really like that. Others like the more traditional. God has gifted us with music in the church. I am delighted. Music really ministers to me. But I know that that's not the bottom line. The question is, does it help God's people do justice and righteousness?

We are presently in the midst of a building program. The plans look wonderful. We will rejoice when we can move back into the sanctuary and listen to our pipe organ once again. There will be room for everyone. But what's the bottom line? If the new building does not help us produce justice and righteousness, the ordering of right relationships and resources, it is all for naught.

We have grown in numbers. These past three years our budget has increased. The cash flow is stable and healthy so that we have been able to enlarge our ministry — add staff — give more to benevolence. People are learning to tithe. Our offerings look good. But that's not the bottom line. The question is, has this growth enlarged our ministry of justice and righteousness? Grapes may all look alike, but some are wild, bitter, unacceptable to God.

Let me share with you two stories that I believe help us to understand mishpat and zedekah, justice and righteousness. The first is about Oscar Romero. He was made Bishop in El Salvador because everyone thought he was conservative and would bring stability to the war-torn country. Soon after he was installed, a priest who was a close friend was killed because he helped the peasants start a cooperative. His friend was a special friend to the poor. Soon the killing of priests and innocent people got worse. Oscar Romero began to see the need for justice. He spoke out against the injustices to the poor. He defended the rights of those who were exploited. He wrote an open letter to U.S. President Jimmy Carter asking him to stop the flow of weapons to El Salvador which were only increasing the bloodshed. He asked soldiers in the El Salvadoran army to refuse to kill their fellow citizens. The Bishop knew what mishpat and zedekah were about. Soon after he took this stand for the poor, Bishop Romero was assassinated while leading the Mass. Oscar Romero discovered what the bottom line was. It was justice and righteousness, working for the reordering of relationships and resources.

The second story is from the Bible. Jesus didn't want people to miss what he meant when he said, "Seek first the kingdom and God's justice" (mishpat and zedekah) so he told them that one day there will be a final judgment. "God will gather all nations. God will say to those on the right, 'Come, blessed by my father. Inherit the kingdom. For I was hungry and you fed me. I was thirsty and you gave me to drink. I was naked and you clothed me, in prison and you visited me, a stranger and you welcomed me. As you have done it unto the least of these you have done it unto me.' "

In telling this story, Jesus helped his listeners to know what the bottom line is. Each Sunday we gather beneath the cross of Jesus we are reminded that the bottom line is about love, love that is willing to sacrifice in order to bring about mishpat and zedekah, justice and righteousness. Amen.

Proper 23 — Matthew 22:1-14
Pentecost 21 — Matthew 22:1-10 (11-14)
Ordinary Time 28 — Matthew 22:1-14

Have You Accepted Jesus' Invitation?

This morning I want to talk to you about becoming a Christian — the invitation of Jesus to come and follow him. It is not my intention to judge who is or is not a Christian, or criticize anyone's experience of salvation, or to suggest that you are not already a member of God's family. My intention is rather to allow this text to speak clearly to us about Jesus' invitation. My purpose is to give voice to Jesus' call to discipleship.

I approach this text from Matthew with a few assumptions, a few underlying givens. Let me share with you what they are.

1. Our text suggests that Jesus invites people to join him — to come to the marriage feast. *I believe that Jesus still invites people to the marriage feast.* That marriage feast is the life of following Christ, the experience of committing your life to God, of being saved from the power of sin, the experience of grace, the experience of being born anew. The call to follow is still being heard. The power of God to change people is still operative and available today as it was when Jesus told this parable.

I believe the Holy Spirit is leading people from darkness to light. "There is being added to the church day by day those who are being saved." God is still in the business of converting, changing people, calling people to leave their nets and follow. The invitation to the marriage feast needs to be heard today as much as it did 2,000 years ago.

E. Stanley Jones, one of this century's greatest missionaries, reminds us that the church will never outgrow the necessity of producing conversions. I strongly believe that. Every time I step into this pulpit, I do so with the expectation that God will call people to become Christians, to repent and believe the gospel. I believe there are people sitting here this morning who will experience in a very real way the call to become a Christian. Jesus is still inviting people to the marriage feast.

2. Another assumption, a given, a basis from which I speak: *I believe that there are still those who will not come,* who have not accepted the invitation, who make light of the invitation as the text suggests. There are in our midst those who are too busy with other interests and distractions. They don't take it seriously. They put off accepting the invitation. There are all kinds of reasons, but the fact is, some are present who have not come to the marriage feast, or they may come but without a wedding garment. They may come to church. They may believe in God. They may say their prayers. But they are not part of the marriage feast. That is, they have not accepted the invitation to come and follow Jesus. They have not known what it means to be saved by grace, to believe in Jesus, to be born again. There has been no commitment of the heart.

We live in an environment within the church where we sometimes assume that everyone is a Christian. Most of us have been baptized and confirmed. We all know John 3:16 and the Lord's Prayer. But that doesn't mean all of us have accepted the invitation to the marriage feast. There are those who do not have on the wedding garment. They mingle among the Christians. They know the party line, but something is missing.

So I enter this pulpit with the assumption that some have yet to accept Christ's invitation to come. Some have not taken it seriously. I don't know who you are, but you do and God does. Today you will hear the invitation once again.

3. Another assumption or maybe a hunch I have this morning is that *some don't know how to accept the invitation.* You

28

are still asking, what does it mean to be a Christian, a follower of Jesus? How do I become a Christian?

I'll never forget my senior sermon at the seminary. Everyone wanted to do their best for our last homiletics class. We were graduating and soon to be ordained pastors. My assignment was a text that dealt with prayer. I prepared well. I thought I did okay. Then came the time for the critique. All my classmates gave their comments. Most of them were very encouraging. I was pleased. Then my homiletics professor, Dr. Halvorson, gave his critique, and I'll never forget it. He said, "George, you preached a good sermon, but something was missing. You showed us a beautiful place to be. That place was a life of prayer. You told us what that place could do for us. You made it very attractive, but you didn't tell us how to get there." He was right.

I wonder if I have been guilty of the same thing in talking about becoming a Christian, a follower of Jesus. I may have described what it means to be a Christian, a beautiful picture. But have I missed telling people how to get there, how to accept the invitation? Do I take for granted that people know how to get there?

So I assume this morning that some of you are waiting for the invitation to be given to you clearly. Some have never realized that they need to respond to the invitation. Some have received bad information about the invitation, the marriage feast. That is, they may think of it more as a walk through the desert than an invitation to a marriage feast. They have listened to the wrong reports.

Some have made light of it because they don't believe there is any hope for them. They have gone too far in rejecting the invitation to a marriage feast. They have listened to the wrong reports.

Some have gone too far in rejecting the invitation. Their sin is too great. Their background is too awful. Their heart is too hard. Their temptations are too strong. Perhaps their own negative self-image keeps them from taking seriously the invitation to follow Jesus. They don't really believe that

God's grace can be so free, so accepting, so forgiving. If you are among this group, I assume that you need help in knowing how to accept the invitation of Jesus.

4. Another assumption I begin with is that *if you reject the invitation long enough, there will come a time when it is too late.* In this parable that Jesus told, the king sent out his servants to call those who were invited. Some would not come. Remember now, a parable is a story meant to get across an important truth. He sent other servants to call them, to plead with them to come.

The king didn't give up after the initial rejection. He gave them another chance. Perhaps a new voice, a different approach would convince them. But when they continually rejected the invitation, the king became very angry and he destroyed the whole city and turned to others with the invitation. To continually reject God's invitation to follow Jesus is very dangerous and risky. Because there will come a time when it is too late. Today is the day of salvation.

Those without a wedding garment will be thrown out. There will be weeping and gnashing of teeth. Jesus ends by saying, "many are called, but few are chosen." Only those who accept the invitation are chosen.

What I'm saying is: *it's urgent business.* It's not something to put off. If you reject the invitation, you run the risk of bringing upon yourself the judgment of God. I don't know what form that judgment will take, but it will come. If you believe in the promise of God for your salvation, you can also believe that he will keep his promise about judgment. As one Baptist preacher said, "If God meant anything, God meant everything."

So let's review. Today's sermon operates with the assumptions that:

1. God is still inviting people to the marriage feast. The Holy Spirit is still calling people to follow Jesus. God may be calling you.

2. Some have yet to accept the invitation. There are still those who make light of it or are too busy. Therefore, the call to accept needs to be heard.

3. Some have never clearly understood how to accept that invitation, how to become a Christian.

4. There will be a time when it is too late. If you reject continually, there will be a time when the door will be shut. There are serious consequences to rejecting the invitation. From this perspective I now proceed to talk about becoming a Christian.

Jesus Invites Us To A Different Way

I want to be as clear as possible in what I say, so listen carefully. If your mind has been wandering, I invite you back.

The invitation to the marriage feast is God's invitation to follow Jesus. It is God saying I want to show you my love, my plan for all people and all creation to live in harmony. I want to show you a different way to wholeness, to health, to meaning and purpose. "Come to me," says Jesus, "and I will give you rest." That rest means rest from a life of toil and struggle that doesn't seem to make a difference. It is a call to the kingdom, the reign of God. It is new and different.

— The world says — domination, accumulation and consumption is the way. Get all you can get.

God says — I invite you to another way.

— The world says — conquer, control, compete.

God says — I invite you to another way.

— The world says — an eye for an eye, get revenge, resist evil with evil.

God says — I invite you to another way.

— The world says — conform, be part of the majority, agree with the masses, go with the flow.

God says — I invite you to another way.

The invitation is an invitation to a marriage feast not a desert experience. That means the kingdom is about love and laughter. It means grace and forgiveness. It means partnership and harmony. God wants you to know and experience unconditional acceptance. God wants to put loving arms

31

around you. God wants to lift you up out of the miry clay you are in. God wants to forgive you. God wants to free you from bondage and guilt. God wants to give you rest.

If there is bitterness in your heart, God wants to take that bitterness away. If there is no joy in your life, God wants to bring laughter. If there is regret or shame, God wants to wash it away. God will remember your sin no more. If you are living under the power of sin, if you are driven, addicted, captive to another allegiance, bound by another strong attraction that is destroying you, God wants to release you, set you free, give you a fresh start. It is God's will that you experience wholeness. It is beautiful, like a marriage feast.

How do you accept this invitation?

1. *Be obedient to the call.* Say a decisive Yes. The Holy Spirit will work in your heart, in your conscience, in your inner self. There will be a nudge, a hunger, a desire to be different, a longing for change. Your conscience will give you a reminder that the way you are going is wrong, a dead end. Something is missing.

Be obedient to that call. Answer Yes. Say it out loud. Say it clearly, decisively. Tell God, "I want to accept your invitation. Just as I am, I come." It might help to go home, get on your knees, or go for a walk and tell God out loud: "I accept your invitation." Or come to the altar here later this morning and pray that prayer. Declare a clear yes to the invitation.

2. *Let go in order to come.* There is a kind of natural resistance to this invitation. Attractive persuasions distract us, lure us away, hold us down. Our sins keep a strong hold on us. When Jesus invites us to come, he invites us to repent. That means to let go of our sins, let go of our excuses, let go of other allegiances, our pretending. Let go of trying to serve two masters.

Come in honesty. Come with your brokenness. Confess to God, I have sinned. I have been hiding, pretending. I want to be changed. One of the first steps in the Alcoholics Anonymous progam is to recognize one's need. That same honesty is important in the call to follow Jesus. Without it all of our intentions fall short.

3. *Receive God's unconditional love.* Let God love you the way you are. Don't try to be good enough. Don't wait until you are good enough. Don't compare with others, measure your worthiness, or look to see if others are coming with you. Just come to the banquet. Receive God's love. Enjoy grace.

It is God's love that will transform you, not your promise to be good. It is God's love that will wash your eyes. It is God's love that will empower you to follow, not your down payment of a good life. It is God's love that will give you that sense of being forgiven, not your good grades in behavior. The hymn says it so well, "Just as I am, I come."

4. *Take hold of someone's hand as you come.* To accept the invitation to the marriage feast is to come into a fellowship with others. We don't have a private room by ourselves at this feast. At this celebration we will belong to a family. We will discover others who are broken, others who are in the process of finding wholeness. The invitation is an invitation to live in community.

Find someone you can hold hands with. By that I mean talk to someone about your decision, your struggle, your joys. Ask for help in following Jesus. Find a companion, a friend or friends, who will support you, pray for you, help you to be accountable. Being a Christian is personal, but it is not private. Hold someone's hand. Find a friend by being a friend. This is where the church can be of help to you. You don't have to tell the world, but tell someone.

5. If you want to follow Jesus, *then follow him;* not just believe, but follow. You learn what that means in the book called the Bible. The invitation to the marriage feast is not to a cheering section sitting in the bleachers or to a good ol' boys club. It is not a rest stop, but it is an invitation to a movement, to a mission to change the world. So if you and I want to take the call seriously we will find some disciplines are important. The Bible needs to be our constant companion. We will give a priority to this operations manual. Let the scriptures be a source of learning how to follow.

In conclusion I want to urge each of us to think about this invitation. Have we accepted this invitation to the marriage feast? Have we responded with a clear and decisive yes?

There was a doctor who received a call late at night to come to the hospital. Someone was near death and needed a physician's attention or death was certain. The hospital was 30 miles away in another town. The doctor dressed and took off in his car. At a stoplight a man jumped into his car, pulled a gun, and told the doctor to get out. "I need your car. Get out," was all he said. The doctor got out and had to find another way to get to the hospital. When he finally arrived the nurse met him and told him the woman just died. "You are too late, Doctor. But would you go and say a word to the husband. He is weeping uncontrollably in the family lounge." When the doctor entered the lounge he found the husband in a corner. To his great surprise he discovered that the husband was the very man who pulled the gun on him because he needed his car.

Sometimes we push out of our lives the very thing that can help us. It might be the church, it might be the Bible, Christian friends, a nudge to make a clear commitment. It might be taking the step of accepting the invitation to the marriage feast.

I encourage you this morning to be obedient to the call. Let go of that which may be holding you back. Be honest before God. Receive God's unconditional love. Come just as you are. Take hold of someone's hand. We need each other. And begin a disciplined plan to read and study God's way found in the Bible.

Don't push out of your life the invitation from the one who can give you life. Amen.

Proper 24 — Matthew 22:15-22
Pentecost 22 — Matthew 22:15-21
Ordinary Time 29 — Matthew 22:15-21

When Is Patriotism An Idol?

Almost everyone who has been brought up in the church has heard of the "taxes to Caesar" story. "Is it right to pay taxes to Caesar?" they asked Jesus. Allegiance to the empire and to God is the issue. Jesus' patriotism is being called into question. I want to talk to you about when patriotism becomes an idol.

The setting is important. It was toward the end of Jesus' ministry, just before his death. His vision was focused. He was going to Jerusalem. There he would be confronted with life and death issues. There he would die on the cross. You catch from the teachings of Jesus that surround this text, a kind of urgency, a kind of confrontation with ultimate questions, questions that probe the depth of one's being. There is in the parables and sayings of Jesus at this point, a question of ultimate authority and allegiance. By what criteria or authority do you make decisions, establish values, find meaning and purpose?

In the sayings of Jesus that surround this text, there is also a number of references to the consequences of one's decisions. Jesus is saying that some day we are going to have to answer for what we do, what we decide. We are accountable. Here are some happenings and stories that surround our text:

35

— The money changers are driven out of the temple. Wrong choices regarding economics catch up with you.

— The fig tree is cursed because there is no fruit on it. There is expectation or else.

— Jesus said to the religious leaders of the Israelites — the kingdom of God will be taken away and given to a nation producing fruits of the kingdom. Judgment is real.

— During these closing discourses Jesus talks about the door being shut on the bridesmaids without oil and the goats on the left hearing the words "Depart from me."

— When servants made light of the invitation to the marriage feast, the king was angry and destroyed them all. He then turned to harlots and tax collectors.

This kind of talk sets the stage for the *"taxes to Caesar"* story. What Jesus had been saying challenged the listeners' thinking, their belief system, their traditions, their allegiances, their positions of privilege, their patriotism. Attention was on edge.

Jesus Is Tested Where Vulnerable

So they put Jesus to the test. They wanted to get Jesus to comment and say what they thought he was saying, so they could discredit him, entangle him in his words, prove to the audience that he was a revolutionary that should be silenced. They suspected in their hearts that he was soft on patriotism, so they went after his Achilles' heel.

You can feel the atmosphere. The air is tense with emotion. "What do you mean God may take the kingdom away from us and give it to another nation? Are you suggesting that our faith, our religious values, our leaders are wrong — are misguided — are leading us down the wrong way?" Their conscience is pricked. Their long held traditions are challenged. They are upset because Jesus exposes their hypocrisy, their idolatry.

So they pick an issue he has alluded to and they try to pin him to the wall. Patriotism — that's a sacred cow that he has failed to worship. Let's ask him about allegiance to the empire, to government authority. That will get people stirred up, divided. They'll stop listening to him if we can expose his lack of patriotism. We'll get this radical teacher to say something that will call his patriotism into question. He's been questioning our uncritical acceptance of those in authority — the status quo — the present world order. Let's give him a scenario that will force him to reveal his lack of allegiance to the government, to Caesar.

"Teacher — we know you are true and teach the way of God." Boy, that really sets one up, doesn't it. Teacher, you don't seem to care what the polls say, what popular opinion is. You are not that impressed or care what a person's title is or how many degrees one has or where one hails from. Tell us, is it lawful to pay taxes to Caesar or not?

They knew that Jesus taught a way that was in direct conflict with Caesar on many points. Caesar stood for the sword — conquer, control by violence. Jesus taught non-violence — turn the other cheek, equality among the sexes.

They knew that Jesus taught the way of justice, cooperation and partnership. Caesar stood for power over others, acquisition of wealth, dominance over others and manipulation.

They knew that Jesus was polls apart from Caesar in his teachings about loving one's enemy, suffering on behalf of others, respecting all people.

There was no doubt in their mind where Jesus stood with regard to Caesar and his politics, his economics, his warring madness. So in their crafty manner they plot, "Let's test Jesus to see if he will say it. Let's bring out the implication of his teachings. Then they will accuse him of being unpatriotic." Their question was both cunning and clever. "Tell us, is it . . ."

Jesus Answers Without Answering

Verse 18 shows that Jesus was aware of their malice. He knew the game they were playing, and he tells it like it is.

"Why put me to the test you hypocrites?" I know what you are doing, and I'm not playing your game. *So he proceeds not to answer their question.* That's important to observe from this text. Jesus answers but he does not really answer their question. Noted biblical scholar Norman Gottwold observes that Jesus refuses to give an outright answer. Instead he throws the question back upon the questioners. He doesn't speak his full mind on the topic. They knew where Jesus stood. He knew that they knew where he stood, so he refused to fall into the trap. "Why put me to the test, you hypocrites." He announces to the audience that he's up to their tricks and he won't get sucked in.

Without first understanding this, we may use this text for all kinds of bad theology and faulty interpretation of the Bible. This text has been used by some to defend the separation of church and state. It has been used by some to defend keeping politics out of the church. It has been used by some to defend uncritical allegiance to government authority, even when it goes against your conscience. It has been used by some to defend civil religion, giving divine status to the empire. Few passages in the Bible are more misused than this one.

A faulty interpretation of this text can lead the church into all kinds of behavior that is contrary to the teachings of Jesus. It can leave us with a gospel that is empty of power to change society's exploitation of creation. It can lead Christians into a kind of uncritical submission to any and all authority in violation of one's conscience, a kind of idolatry of the empire. The church has often been unable or unwilling to serve as a social conscience to society because of a faulty interpretation of this text.

What do I mean, Jesus didn't answer the question? He doesn't address what is lawful. They asked, "Is it lawful?" He doesn't answer that. He doesn't say yes. He doesn't say no. Behind the question is the whole idea of Caesar as more than a legitimate authority. Is Caesar an ultimate authority? Are his policies consistent with the values of the kingdom of God? Notice Jesus does not condone or condemn Caesar's policies in his reply. He already established his differences with Caesar in his previous teachings. So with great skill, Jesus answers them without really answering their question. And those who were followers would know what is Caesar's and what is God's, what allegiance is legitimate and what is idolatry.

This is one of those texts where those who are following, those who are listening to the teachings of Jesus — those who are Spirit led — *will know what Jesus was saying because of what he had been saying.* Those who are in tune with what Jesus stood for will marvel at how he answered them without answering their question. On the other hand, those who are religious but not following Jesus may, of course, use Jesus' answer to support any number of beliefs about civil authority and allegiance to the empire.

One Cannot Serve Two Masters

Jesus knew that there is nothing that belongs to Caesar and does not first belong to God. His disciples knew that. He made it clear that you cannot serve two masters. You cannot serve God and money — God and Caesar — God and the empire — God and something else. You have to choose where your ultimate allegiance is.

Whether we pay taxes (money) to Caesar, we must pass the first test: Does this please God? Does this enable me to be faithful to my supreme allegiance, which is the kingdom of God? Does it serve the cause of justice for all God's creation?

Friends, there are not two gods for us. We do not split our ultimate allegiance in two directions. Part of me follows God, part of me follows the empire. Money belongs to Caesar and the Bible belongs to God. On Sunday I listen to God and on Monday I listen to Caesar. That's not what this text suggests in any way, shape or form. We need to come to grips with this as we grapple with life's choices and values. There is nothing, not even taxes or orders from Caesar to go to war, that can escape passing through the test of my allegiance to God, my obedience to my conscience.

The ultimate issue at stake here is the first commandment. You shall have no other gods before me. You shall love the Lord your God with all your heart and mind. If Jesus would have suggested by his answer that some things belong to Caesar, no matter what, it would have been in direct violation of the first commandment. He would have made an idol of patriotism. Nothing belongs to Caesar that does not first and ultimately belong to God. Remembering this helps us see the irony in Jesus' answer.

The Great Temptation

What I want to suggest this morning is that *here is a great temptation we often face.* It is a temptation to violate the first commandment, to have other gods, other allegiances that take precedence over our allegiance to God. Not that we would replace God — or deny God — or stop believing in God. That's not a temptation for most of us. But the great temptation is to put Caesar along side of God, and in essence say — In some things I follow Caesar, in some things I follow my conscience. It is the temptation to serve God and Caesar at the same time with equal or shared authority over our conscience. And let me tell you, it's seductively tempting; it's powerful. Sometimes you don't know you are being tested until it's all over.

When Jesus was tempted to turn stones into bread, when he was tempted to fall down from the temple, to prove the power of God, when he was tempted to bow down for a moment so that his ultimate goal could be achieved, it was no easy decision. There were forces — circumstances and rational arguments for going along with the suggestions. Jesus' temptations were very real. They were tempting.

Patriotism is a good thing. Every nation needs people who are committed to its security, its survival and its well being. It is good and natural to love one's homeland. The question

40

is, when does patriotism become an idol, something that competes with my allegiance to God.

Do you remember the story of Daniel in the lion's den? I loved this story as a child. Have you told it to your children recently? Caesar, who then was called Nebuchadnezzar, had decreed a law that no one should pray to any other god but him. The empire needed a sign of loyalty and a gesture of unity from its citizens. It was a flag waving time. He asked all citizens to give their full allegiance to the empire. Daniel, however, had a higher allegiance. So it was again a question of patriotism — Caesar or God, the power of public policy vs. the individual conscience. I think somehow my Sunday school teachers missed the opportunity to show us children how this story applies to our lives today. I don't remember seeing any danger, any great temptations to give our allegiance to the empire at the cost of violating our conscience. I wasn't helped to see the Nebuchadnezzar is often dressed in the attire of patriotism — national security — economic growth — military might. That, my friend, is the great temptation today. Where is our ultimate allegiance?

You may be tempted to cheat on your income tax.

You may be tempted to cheat on your wife or husband.

You may be tempted to sleep in on Sunday.

You may be tempted to waste your money on the lottery or some other risky venture.

You may be tempted to lie, steal, covet, swear.

But the great temptation, the one that is the ultimate test, the one that shapes everything we do, is the temptation to idolatry. The temptation to have more than one God, to serve two masters. The temptation to give part of our ultimate allegiance to Caesar and part to God. The temptation to bow our knees before two altars — the flag and the cross.

It is a powerful temptation. It is real for every one of us. If we have not wrestled with it, maybe we have already given in to it. If we do not recognize this temptation with its modern application, it may be a sign that we have not come to grips with what it means to follow Jesus. There is strong peer pressure, pressure from our surroundings — popular opinion polls, the need to stay employed. No one wants to be considered unpatriotic, different. Everyone should love and serve their own nation with honor. We are thankful for what our country has given us. Patriotism is good except when it becomes an idol.

There is strong pressure to try to have it both ways. We want God and we want national security and prosperity. We want God and we want the benefits of Caesar's policy. So we try to separate our religion and our politics, our Sundays from our Mondays.

There is strong pressure to delay our decision of ultimate allegiance, put off choosing, being middle of the roaders, being silent, hoping that somehow we won't have to decide, take sides, reveal our true master.

The great temptation — is it God or Caesar that I follow — comes to the surface for us at special moments in our lives. It came in a powerful way to Jesus when he was in the wilderness for 40 days just after his baptism. There are certain moments in life when we are confronted, tested, tempted. Will our ultimate allegiance be to God and the conscience God has given us, or will we divide our allegiance and try to live with two ultimate authorities in order to get along, to avoid conflict. The choices seldom seem to be black and white. We are confronted when we are most vulnerable. It's not easy.

When Jesus withstood the temptation, it says the angels came and ministered to him. God sent his angels to Daniel in the lion's den. I believe that God's angels will minister to you, too, as you withstand the great temptation to bow down to Caesar at the cost of violating your conscience. God's presence will be made real to you.

We need the presence of Jesus given us in the sacrament this morning. Come — receive his body and his blood as he reveals his love to us. Come, experience the presence of angels in the sacrament as Jesus gives himself to us. Come, be empowered to follow your conscience to give your ultimate allegiance to God. Having experienced that touch of God we can go out and love our country, our world by loving God first. Amen.

Proper 25 — Matthew 22:34-46
Pentecost 23 — Matthew 22:34-40 (41-46)
Ordinary Time 30 — Matthew 22:34-40

What Does It Mean To Love?

Do you remember the first time you told a boyfriend or girlfriend those three words, "I love you?" When did you first say it to the one you married? I don't remember the particular occasion, but I remember thinking about it. Do I dare tell her how I feel? I really think I love her, but should I tell her yet? Then I thought, what if she doesn't have any of these feelings for me? Will she be embarrassed? Will I be sticking my neck out? Will it change our relationship if I tell her that I love her? Should I wait until I'm more certain?

That was a long time ago. I still say those words — perhaps not as often as I should. And I still love to hear them said to me, "I love you."

Those three words are powerful. To say them, to hear them said, can make a big difference. Today's children's song sums it up.

Love, love, love, that's what it's all about.
'Cause God loves us we love each other
Mother, Father, Sister, Brother
Everybody sing and shout
'Cause that's what it's all about
It's about love, love, love
It's about love, love, love.

43

Jesus said, "No one has greater love than this, to lay down one's life for another person. You shall love God with all your heart, with all your soul, and with all your mind. And you shall love your neighbor as yourself." Love, that's what it's all about. Jesus also said, "I am giving you these so that you may love one another." John's epistle puts it this way, "Beloved, let us love one another because love is from God; everyone who loves is born of God and knows God. Whoever does not love does not know God, for God is love." John also says, "If we love one another, God lives in us and God's love is perfected in us. God is love. Those who abide in love abide in God and God abides in them."

Here we have several statements about love. It seems pretty obvious that the central teaching of Jesus is love. The kingdom of God is about love. Justice and righteousness are about love. It starts out with love. Love is the energy that keeps us alive, and love is the goal. If there is a God, it doesn't say God loves, but God is love. The essence of God is love. The prime mover, the creator, the mastermind behind all that we see and discover is love. The manifestation of that love came in the person of Jesus. God sent the one born of Mary to reveal, to let us see love. God wanted to love us in a tangible way, so Jesus was born. The Word of God which is love became flesh.

In the life of Jesus we see that love is a binding relationship, a caring, a willingness to sacrifice, to lay down one's life, to enter into the other person's situation. "Greater love has no one," says Jesus, "than to lay down one's life for others." Jesus' life is a demonstration of that love.

In the end, the bottom line is: God wants us to love one another. It's God's commandment to us. Love sums up all the commandments. It has authority behind it. It's not an option. It's not a theory, an idea, a philosophy to bounce around. It's not a question or suggestion as one possible route you may take. It's a command. This is my commandment that you love one another. It is the "law," that the psalmist meditates on day and night (Psalm 1).

There is some interesting insight in 1 John that may bother some of us a bit, especially those who operate with a rather closed system. It says, "Whoever loves is born of God and knows God. Those who abide in love abide in God."

We tend to turn it around. We say whoever is born of God, loves. Or if you accept Christ as your Savior, if you abide in God, then you will love. John doesn't use that formula here. He says, "Whoever loves is born of God."

Baptism, justification by faith, saved by grace, accepting Christ, or being accepted by God is not mentioned here. Being a member of a church, or believing the Bible to be God's word, or being heterosexual, or believing certain dogmas, none of these is mentioned here. But "Whoever loves is born of God."

It raises some interesting questions about our attitude toward people who aren't inside our circle. Jews, Arabs, Moslems, atheists, people who believe differently than we do. We don't have time to deal with all the implications of this, but I draw your attention to it so that we don't become too narrow or dogmatic in our judgment or attitude toward others. "Whoever loves is born of God and knows God." If we don't like this verse, if it unsettles our theology, then of course we can ignore it or cross it out and move on to some other parts of the Bible that we feel more comfortable with. However, it can be a rather liberating insight from God's Word. When asked to summarize what the will of God is all about, Jesus puts it simply. Love God and love your neighbor.

My point is, love seems to be the beginning and the end, the top line and the bottom line. So we sing, "Love, love, love, that's what it's all about." But that's not all the Bible says. That's not all that Jesus said. He goes on to say more and to demonstrate what he means. As we study the scriptures and as we live out our faith we discover some interesting things about love.

Love is more than a feeling. It is an attitude from which we operate. It is a way of behaving toward others. We may not always feel love, but we can do the loving thing.

Can you think of someone at work or one of your relatives that you don't feel loving towards? I'm sure we all can. Your feelings toward that person are perhaps negative or suspicious. You may have been hurt by that person. Their words may have cut you down. They don't deserve your love. God has given you a command to love that person. That doesn't mean that you have to feel a certain way, but to do the loving thing, to respond from a stance of love. That might mean to forgive, to give that person another chance, to sacrifice your pride. It might mean deciding not to pay that person back or putting them down in order to prove that you are right. You may decide not to criticize or talk about that person behind their back.

We don't have to wait for a feeling of love before we love. We can decide to love without feeling love. I encourage you to think about that person you don't feel good about. The presence of God in you will help you to love that person. It may not change that person, but it will change you. Love is more than a feeling. It's an attitude, a stance from which we see and operate.

Love is more than a doctrine. It is an experience. Children who grow up with little love in their homes may have a hard time loving others. It is being loved that enables us to love. "Beloved, since God loved us so much we are to love one another." It begins with the experience of love. It is being loved that can change our behavior.

Dennis was a neighbor boy when we lived in San Francisco. He was always getting into trouble, doing the wrong thing. His mother found out that he had broken our basement window and crawled in one day when we were not home. She marched him over to our house to apologize. Dennis looked frightened as he came down to my office which was in the basement of our home at that time. He didn't speak, but his lips quivered. I didn't speak either. Instead, I took his arm and put him in my lap. I hugged him and told him that I loved him. He started to sob. The hard shell he had usually displayed started to crack. At other times when I tried to scold him or preach to him about what was right, it didn't seem to work. Once Dennis experienced love, it made a difference. Love is more than a doctrine. It is an experience.

Love is more than words. It is action. I can say I love you to my wife, my children, or my friend. But if it doesn't show in my behavior, then my words become like a noisy gong or a clanging cymbal. We can say that we believe in God, that we believe the Bible, that we are forgiven sinners, that we are followers of Jesus, but the test of reality comes not in our words, but in the way we live. We can say we trust God to take care of us, that we don't have other gods, that we love to tell the story. But the real test of love is not in our words. It is in our action.

The Bible is very practical. For example, to help us know what it means to love our neighbor, the Bible talks about giving a tithe — 10 percent of all our income to the Lord's work to the poor. It is for others (Malachi 3:8-10). The tithe is not an amount, but a percentage, a step toward equality, toward redistribution. It may be a sacrifice to do that, but to love is a sacrifice.

Some of us have adopted a lifestyle that makes tithing very difficult. That is, we have homes, cars, clothes, sports and long range goals that make it difficult to live on the 90 percent. So we may take from the 10 percent that belongs to God for our lifestyle, to meet our obligations and appetites, to fulfill our goals. The Bible says that is stealing from God. It is the failure to love that leads us to steal what does not belong to us. Of course, parents who steal may find that their children will also learn to steal.

Tithing is not about church budgets, building programs, or stewardship campaigns. It's about love. It's about the commandment to love as God loved us. The scriptures say, "Let us not love in word but in deed and in truth." Some of us will go fishing next weekend because it's the season opener.

47

Or we may get tickets to the ballgame or the concert. Cultural events are important and good. It might be a sign of love if we make sure that we have taken our tithe out first.

Love is more than words. Love is sacrifice, obedience, partnership, turning the other cheek. We may sing "I love to tell the story of unseen things above," but what the world is looking for is not words or melodies, but love, love that manifests itself in the way we spend our money, the way we vote, the way we treat those who don't deserve our love, those whose skin color or beliefs are different than ours. "Mother, father, sister, brother, everybody sing and shout, 'cause that's what it's all about. It's about love."

To love is not always easy, but as the Bible says, it does make our joy complete. If Jesus taught us anything, he taught us that to love can be painful.

The movie *The Nasty Girl*, is a German film with subtitles. It's about a young girl who decides to write an essay for school about her home town in Germany. She concentrates on her home town during World War II. She is commended and applauded by the residents of her community until she begins to discover some covered-up history. People had forgotten their town's treatment of Jews. The secret files of that history were locked up, off limits. People remembered only what they wanted to remember. It's no different today. But the young girl persists. She doesn't quit even though everyone tells her to drop it. She marries one of her high school teachers, and continues her research into the town's history. After some time, even her own husband turns against her. She feels alone, forsaken, even hated as someone throws a fire bomb into her apartment. They call her a communist. She is the "nasty girl" in town because of her persistent quest for the truth. Her love for the truth, her love for justice, compels her to go forward until she finally is able to tell the full story. It is a painful story to watch as it unfolds on the screen. One is reminded how the love of truth and justice can be very painful. Jesus' example certainly teaches this.

But not to love is to deny who we are.

Not to love is to lose the joy of living.

Not to love is to live a very lonely life.

Not to love is boring and dull.

Not to love is to merely exist, without meaning or purpose.

Not to love is to deny the presence of God, the image of God within us.

Not to love is a form of atheism.

We come together each week not because we have to go to "church" to be Christian or to get to heaven. We come together to experience God's love in a fresh way, to explore what it means to love, to find energy in order to love. We come so we can be obedient to the command, to love God with all our hearts, and to love our neighbor as ourselves so that our joy may be complete. Every Sunday is a love feast. Every day of the week is filled with opportunities to love and to be loved. Amen.

What Is Servant Leadership?

I have been interviewed by a few call committees during my 31 years of ministry. It's always been a good experience. You know that they want to get to know as much about you as they can in the brief time you have together. Whether you are interested in the call or not, you try to be honest and fair but careful in your answers and comments. Many of you have interviewed for jobs and you know what it's like.

Most church call committees have discussed beforehand what the needs of the congregation are. They are looking for certain qualities or gifts that will fit their needs. High on the list are usually preaching, administration, evangelism, youth ministry and budget management. Sometimes they are looking for someone who is musical or married or experienced or energetic or a good counselor. Almost always a call committee has on their list or implied in their search, a person who is committed to the gospel of Jesus, a devout Christian.

Once in a while you will find a call committee that is looking for a pastor who is a servant. Not very often does the servant concept surface in surveys taken among members as to what they think the call committee should look for. It is seldom on any printed list of priorities. Perhaps it is mostly assumed. Of course, our new pastor must wear the mantle of

51

being a servant. Isn't that a "given" for any Christian leader, for any Christian?

Jesus discovered a lack of servant leadership among the scribes and Pharisees of his day. It really bothered him. He comes back to it again and again in his preaching and teaching. Jesus calls them hypocrites, blind guides, fools, whitewashed tombs, a brood of vipers. At times, he was very blunt. He said to the Sadducees, "You are wrong. You know neither the scripture nor the power of God." In other words, you are operating from a lousy theology. People look to you for leadership and guidance, but your interpretation of the Bible is wrong and your understanding of God is off base. Some of the toughest resistance that Jesus faced came from religious leadership.

The text from Matthew gives us some insight into what Jesus saw lacking among the religious leaders. Keep in mind that leadership here is not limited to what we could call clergy. Scribes and Pharisees were not the priests in the temple but lay leaders who lived very disciplined lives. They were the ones with religious authority. People looked to them for spiritual guidance and as models. Here is a list of Jesus' criticisms about religious leadership in his day:

They did not practice what they taught (hypocrisy).

They put heavy burdens on others but not themselves (legalism).

They sought and loved public recognition (pride).

Status, respect and titles were important to them (arrogance).

They locked people out of the kingdom (judgmental).

They established laws to benefit themselves (greed).

They neglected to emphasize justice and mercy (bias).

They were accomplices to silencing the prophets (oppressive).

The list goes on in the whole 23rd chapter. It is very extensive and critical. We see here a side of Jesus that is often left out of our story books and Sunday school lessons. There is a pivotal verse that comes right in the middle of this discourse

52

by Jesus, and it is found at the end of our assigned lesson for today. It says, "The greatest among you will be your servant."

What does it mean to be a servant? What is servant leadership? It is not only an issue for call committees to consider as they look for pastoral leadership, it is a quality to be sought by all who follow Jesus, and certainly is desirable in local church leadership and the institutional church.

When this community thinks about our church, hopefully they think of us as a servant. "The greatest among you will be your servant." It is a different attitude than what we learn from a society that is fueled by greed, competition and dominance. Servant leadership is certainly counter-cultural, and therefore, meets strong resistance both from within and without.

Jesus is greatly disturbed by hypocrisy among leaders. He uses some of his harshest words for those who teach and lead, but do not practice what they teach. You hypocrites, he calls them. And then he gives several examples of their hypocrisy.

Hypocrisy is a common problem in all religions, in all churches, and in every Christian's life. It's never easy to live up to one's beliefs. Others can always find inconsistency and failure to do what we profess to be.

We believe in the 10 commandments. We accept them as a guide for our behavior, but don't always obey them. It's hard to get a passing grade on the first commandment. "You shall have no other gods before me." We claim to follow Jesus, but sometimes we don't. We teach love, but there are times when love is not evident in our behavior. We tell people not to judge others, but we end up judging. Jesus said to take the log out of your eye before you try taking the speck out of your neighbor's eye. Who has not used this quote from Jesus to get people off our backs when we feel judged, to expose hypocrisy?

Hypocrisy is very real, very present, and potentially very harmful to the witness of the gospel. Some, of course, will look for it in others as a way to excuse themselves from their irresponsibility or disobedient behavior. I know so and so who claims to be a Christian, and I've seen them do worse things than I do. Or, I don't attend worship at church because there are too many hypocrites there.

A young teenage girl was captured by the message of Jesus. She came regularly and on her own to worship, and never missed a confirmation class. Discipleship was something she was attracted to. Her parents came only at Easter and Christmas. Once when this daughter did something that was a direct violation of obedience to her parents, they scolded her and accused her of being a hypocrite. "You go to church and claim to be so religious, but see what good it does you." The young girl was crushed and wondered if she should quit attending things at her church. Hypocrisy was used by the parents to justify their lack of commitment to discipleship.

I like the phrase, "The church is not a museum of saints. It is, rather, a hospital for sinners." What binds us together is not our accomplishments but our common brokenness, our need for love and forgiveness and our allegiance to Jesus Christ.

To be a servant church or a servant leader means to model a sense of love and acceptance toward others. People look for models to follow. A child looks for a model in learning how to live as a baptized child of God.

If the church and its leaders talk about love and acceptance but do not practice it, then we are in trouble and in need of repentance or new leadership. I close by reading a true story shared by someone who experienced first hand what our text is talking about. The story is titled, *A Brief Encounter*.

It was an extraordinary experience. While attending a conference at a local church, I slipped out to the hall to make a phone call relating to my work. The operator put me on "hold" and my mind drifted to two women having a conversation across the hall. "The church really needs to do something about homosexuality," one stated loudly. "I heard the worst sermon last Sunday. We attended a church where the pastor said in his sermon that it's okay to be homesexual! Can you imagine a pastor saying that?"

My interest piqued, but the telephone operator drew me back to the phone, and the women were gone by the time I was done. However, a few minutes later, while turning a corner in the hallway, I came face-to-face with the woman I'd overheard.

"Excuse me," I ventured. "I believe I overheard a conversation you were having regarding a sermon you heard. I'm interested in what you were saying, and wonder if you would care to talk about it. Do you have time?"

Responding eagerly to my request, she began, "Oh yes, I was talking about a sermon I heard last Sunday. Not at this church; we're members here. It was at another church. The pastor said it's okay to be homosexual. Can you imagine? It was Easter Sunday and the sermon had nothing to do with Easter. It wasn't biblical at all. He talked about divorce and unhappy marriages, about being single and about oppressed people. And he said something about sexual orientation. It was so depressing and had nothing to do with Easter."

"How did you happen to attend that church on Easter?" I asked.

"My relatives go there, so we went with them. That church has had a terrible time. The last pastor was into social issues . . . and now this one! He's a man in his 50s and a pastor of the same church body as we are. He shouldn't be allowed to be a pastor! He didn't even preach from the Bible."

In the face of her anger, I said timidly, "I think I heard the same sermon."

"Really, you were there? Wasn't it terrible?"

"For me it was different than what you've said." I paused, searching for words to express myself. "It was very biblical. The pastor used the scripture about the two women going to the tomb of Jesus, and they wondered 'Who will roll away the stone?' He applied that to our lives by asking, 'Who will roll away the stone in our lives?' "

With her eyes fastened on mine, I continued, "The pastor suggested some problem areas in people's lives. He said some in the congregation may be experiencing an unhappy marriage

55

where the gleam in a wife's eyes has left when she looks at her husband. Others may be single — not because of choice — but because of divorce. 'Or,' he said, 'it could be that some of you are single due to your sexual orientation and may feel rejected by society and are lonely. Others in our world may be oppressed or hungry and need that stone rolled away.' The pastor continued to mention several problems and then said, 'Whatever our needs, the good news is that God who raised Jesus from the dead is the one who rolls away the stone.' He went on to list ways that we can be closer to God and have the stones in our lives rolled away.''

Though I didn't continue to elaborate on the sermon, I could have reminded her of the pastor's emphasis on the resurrection of Jesus as the basis for our hope and new life in Christ. But, feeling I'd detained her long enough, I concluded by saying, ''I found it very helpful and biblical.''

''You did?'' her voice and face expressing disbelief. ''Well, I asked my husband after the service, 'Did you hear him say that homosexuality is okay?' He agreed that we had. And our daughter who is a teenager, even she said, 'He's not a Christian!' ''

With knees shaking and a voice barely louder than a whisper, I responded, ''I know that pastor, and I know he's a deeply committed Christian. Even though you don't accept him, he would be very accepting of you. I know, because he's my husband.'' No longer able to hold back the tears, I stood crying before her.

Shock filled her face; with wet eyes she uttered, ''I'm sorry.'' Putting her hand on my shoulder, she said, ''It's just that we're so used to our church. We just talk about love.''

''I'm sorry, too,'' I replied softly. ''I'm not angry at you. But, I'm very sad. Christians need to learn to love and accept one another — even when we disagree. It's important, I think, that we not be judgmental. I'm judgmental at times, also. It makes me very sad.''

We awkwardly shared a gentle hug, parted, and went our ways. It was an extraordinary experience.

Jesus said, "The greatest among you will be your servant. Whoever exalts themselves will be humbled and all who humble themselves will be exalted." Amen.

How Does One Prepare For The Unknown?

What is one of the most foolish things you have ever done? Pay good money for a suit or dress that you never wore? Buy a car that turned out to be a lemon? Invest your savings based on good advice, but end up losing it all? Have an affair that you thought would be brief and secret, but turned out to bring havoc on everything?

But who likes to be reminded of one's foolishness? What is one of the wisest things you have ever done?

Saying "yes" to the one you married, or "no" to the one you almost married? Was it admitting that you were helpless over the power of alcohol and finally going to AA? Was it deciding to put away some savings out of every paycheck when you first started to earn a salary? Was it changing jobs, changing friends, changing lifestyles? Was it turning your life over to God?

It might be interesting to gather in clusters and share our stories of foolish things and wise things we have done. In our text, Jesus tells a story about 10 bridesmaids. Five were wise and five were foolish. In reading this parable, we are also reminded of the story in the Sermon on the Mount where Jesus told about the wise person who built a house on a rock, a solid foundation, and a foolish person who built on sand. Of course,

59

the house built on the sand fell to pieces when the rains came because the foundation was not right. The wise person, whose house did not fall, was like the person who hears the Word and does what it says. In both this story and in today's text the world seems to be made up of wise and foolish people.

In the story of the bridesmaids, the issue of wisdom and foolishness is preparedness . . . being ready. Maybe the founder of the scouting movement was familiar with this parable when it was decided that the scouts' motto would be "Be Prepared." There were five bridesmaids who took enough oil and were therefore ready when the bridegroom came. Five others were not prepared. They did not take enough oil for their lamps. So they missed out on that great opportunity when the critical moment arrived. Jesus is telling his disciples to be prepared. Don't be foolish. Be ready at all times. We ask, be ready for what? What does having oil in one's lamp mean?

The church has always looked upon this passage as a strong warning to be ready for the day of judgment, the return of Christ, the end of time, one's own death or whatever language we may use. Part of our gospel proclamation includes the message that Jesus "will come again to judge the living and the dead." The scriptures clearly teach that there will be a judgment day, a day of accounting. In spite of all the misuse of that teaching, we would do well to keep in mind that which we confess in the Apostles' Creed, "Jesus will come again to judge the living and the dead."

It is important to be ready for that final hour whether it takes place when we die or when God chooses to appear in some dramatic form to execute judgment. I have to admit I don't understand very much about the end, or the rapture, or the apocalypse as it is called. In my lifetime I've encountered many bizarre attempts to interpret the end times. Few have been helpful to me. I have become weary of them. It is enough for me to know that God is in charge and that we are held accountable. Some day God will bring to completion what has been set toward a goal. Justice and righteousness will prevail in the end. But there will be a time when the door will be shut and it will be too late . . . too late to get ready. People of faith should never take lightly the place of judgment in their understanding of God.

We need not limit our readiness to the final hour, the last judgment. God comes into our lives in the present situation at special times, at special moments. Sometimes we encounter the bridegroom when we least expect it. We are encouraged to live so that whenever we experience that moment of opportunity — that moment of truth — that moment of encounter or challenge — we will be prepared. We will be ready. We need oil in our lamps, at all times, not just at the end of time.

Take an athletic team, for example. Very often there is the top prize for which they strive. The Super Bowl in football, the Stanley Cup in hockey, the World Series in baseball. There is a "final hour" that every team strives toward. But their readiness better not be limited to the Super Bowl, the Stanley Cup finals or the World Series. The team needs to be ready for each week, each game, each encounter. You and I know what happens when a team looks beyond the next game to the big one and forgets to be ready for the present challenge.

The wise are those who are ready at all times for the moment when our lamps are needed — lamps with oil, lest we encounter an unexpected visitation, a moment of truth. Behold! The bridegroom cometh! Those moments may take us by surprise, and it's too late to run off to the store and get some oil.

The phone rings. It's the hospital. Your son/daughter has been in an accident and the future you had imagined for them is cut short. How can you face it? There's no time to run off and get some oil. No time to prepare. The bridegroom cometh!

The pink slip arrives on your desk. You've just been notified that you've lost your job, suddenly, after 25 years. No warning. Someone watches as you clear your desk, and they usher you out to your car. You can't believe it. What will you tell your spouse, your children? You are crushed. It's too late to run off and get some oil. No time to prepare. The bridegroom cometh!

One day you wake up with an ultimatum — either you get help for your drinking problem or your marriage is over. You never thought it would turn out this way. You were convinced you could handle your drinking habits. You love your spouse, your children. Tomorrow was always going to be different. But suddenly, the possibility of losing your spouse, your children, everything you've lived for is real, and it's too late to run off and get some oil. And no one else's oil can work in your lamp. No time to prepare. The bridegroom cometh!

As a teenager, friends are important to you, but all of a sudden the one you considered your best friend turns against you. That person you trusted tells lies about you. You are deeply hurt, tempted to really get even. You can't believe that your best friend would do that. Now what? It's too late to run off and get oil for your lamp. No time to prepare. The bridegroom cometh!

Moments come when the only thing we have to fall back on is who we are. If there is no oil in our lamps we are left out, nowhere to turn or we end up doing something very foolish.

The story of the wise and foolish bridesmaids is a reminder to be prepared — be ready — for those surprise encounters that will happen, not just at the end, but throughout our lives. Are you ready? Do you have adequate oil in your lamp?

I'd like to suggest some types of encounters we need to be ready for, times when the bridegroom cometh. Such moments often come to us at unexpected times, sometimes in disguise or unannounced, sometimes as interruptions. We can't always predict when these special moments appear, so if we are not living in preparedness, we may find ourselves short of oil and miss the opportunity given to us. We may panic and then find the door is shut.

The Moment Of Temptation

Sometimes temptation comes when you least expect it. You may be doing well. Things are going great. Suddenly and without warning you are face-to-face with temptation. It is powerful. Blinding. Subtle. Seductive. Sometimes it comes most strongly right after you have experienced a special blessing, a mountaintop experience. The temptor makes it sound so reasonable and so good that it doesn't seem like a temptation.

Unless there has been some readiness, some preparation that has taken place, you may well be swept off your feet. By the time you wake up and realize what has happened, the door may be shut.

We all face the temptation to allow good things to rob us of the best. A parent may find advantages in working extra hours, but in so doing neglects time with the children. Later we wake up and wonder how we let it happen. It is subtle and can only be clearly recognized after we've gone through it. Sex is very beautiful, and at the same time, a very powerful force in every human being. We may think we have it under control, but suddenly it surfaces and the temptation is strong to express oneself in a selfish, exploitive, destructive manner. In a very quick moment, the beautiful becomes ugly because we weren't ready for such an encounter.

Greed is often masked as progress, growth or good business sense. We may be riding the wave of success — reaping the rewards of hard work when suddenly and subtly, prosperity turns into greed, wanting more than we need, more than our share, what belongs to someone else. Greed is a powerful temptation that uses many popular and acceptable masks. It is blinding and seductive, especially when we allow the system to be greedy for us.

Only those who are living in a state of alert preparedness are able to withstand the strong pull of evil that lurks close beside us throughout our lives. Be ready, make sure you have enough oil in your lamps for that moment of temptation. Behold the bridegroom cometh.

The Moment Of Decision

Another type of encounter that we need to be ready for is the leadership of true and false prophets. The Bible is constantly talking about false prophets and people with itching ears. Most of us have had people knock on our doors, eager to teach us the truth, ready and trained to lead us with the right questions and pointing to certain Bible verses. As they talk, we may feel cheated by our tradition, our church, for not making it clear to us. Some people are swept off their feet by sincerity, personal attention, knowledge of parts of the Bible and current events. Who do you believe? Who are the true, who are the false teachers, prophets?

Whenever there is a global crisis, especially those that call our attention to the Middle East, we encounter new voices of prophecy . . . people predicting the battle of Armageddon and the period of tribulation. For them it seems so obvious that the Bible is coming true in the drama of current events. "Lo here, Lo there," they say. This one or that one is the antichrist. Drop what you're doing and get ready for the rapture. Book sales on prophecy go sky high during such times. Who do you believe? How can you tell the false prophets from the true prophets?

A Martin Luther King Jr. comes along and challenges the church, the nation, with a wake-up call. None of us are free until all of us are free. "I have a dream," he says. "I say to you my friends that even though we must face the difficulties of today and tomorrow, I still have a dream. It is a dream deeply rooted in the American dream that one day this nation will rise up and live out the true meaning of its creed. We hold these truths to be self evident, that all men and women are created equal." King's speech from the steps of the capitol in Washington, D.C. will always be remembered. It was a new voice, a passionate voice. He went to jail for preaching his message of love and equality. Finally, we killed him. Many in the church wondered about this black man who caused such a stir. As a young pastor, I took our young people to hear him speak to 15,000 youth in Miami Beach. Some parents called me before we left and told me to cancel the trip because King was a communist. They had friends in the FBI and they knew.

Whom do you believe? There are prophets. Some have a message we need to hear and act upon. Some are false prophets. How can you tell the true from the false prophets? There is need to be ready because they appear in unexpected places at moments we have not anticipated. They are not on our agenda. Unless we are living a life of preparedness, we may be led astray or fail to listen to a word that God has for us. Behold the bridegroom cometh.

The Moment Of Jesus' Presence

Another type of blessing or visitation that we may miss if we are not prepared is the presence of Jesus in the lives of those who suffer from hunger, oppression and various forms of injustice. Jesus said, "I was hungry and you fed me . . . in that you did it to the least of these, you did it to me." Some were surprised because they didn't expect to meet Jesus in their encounter with the forgotten ones. In Proverbs we read that to lend to the poor is to lend to the Lord.

God comes to us in different ways. Sometimes in the proclaimed word or the sacraments. God comes through the Bible's message, the scriptures. We encounter God in the voices of nature "when through the woods and forest glades we wander." God also comes to us in the lives of broken people. That person in need has the face of Jesus to the one who is following Christ. We may miss that connection unless we are living in the state of preparedness.

Before going on a trip to Central America to study the reality and causes of hunger and poverty, our leader told us to be ready to encounter Jesus in the lives of the people we would meet. He was right. We did meet Jesus in those people. Not because they were living closer to God than we were, but somehow God has chosen to come to us in the lives of those who are deprived of life's basic necessities. On that trip we learned the truth of Jesus' words, "I was hungry and you fed me."

We come to worship in our church buildings. We make regular visits to the house of the Lord. There we hope to encounter a living God who comes to us in Jesus Christ. We come saying, "We would see Jesus." Perhaps we should also make regular visits to be with the nobodies of society, the forgotten ones. There, too, we would meet the presence of God who has come to us in Jesus Christ. We miss that opportunity unless there is ample oil in our lamps. Behold the bridegroom cometh.

This sermon has been about being ready — living in preparedness — so that when moments of encounter happen, when we are visited by God, we might not miss the opportunity it provides for us to enter the banquet feast. The question this text leaves us with or leads us to is this: What does it mean to be ready? What is this oil needed for our lamps? How do we prepare for the moment, those moments, when the bridegroom comes?

The answer to that is made more clear to us when we link this story with the other story Jesus told about wise and foolish people . . . the one I mentioned at the beginning of this sermon. There Jesus said the wise person is the one who hears my Word and does it. The foolish person, Jesus said, is the one who hears my Words, but does not act on them.

The oil we need is the presence of God manifested and experienced when we are obedient to God's call to love our neighbor, to follow the teachings of Jesus, to trust in the promise. Being ready — preparedness — happens when day-by-day, week-by-week as we hear God's Word and are receptive to God's presence. Our oil is renewed when we are actually doing what God tells us to do. In other words, as we follow Jesus in our daily lives, we are storing up on oil. This following embraces our economics, our politics, our social lives, and our religious lives. It is in doing justice, loving mercy and walking humbly with God that we discover and renew oil in our lamps.

In living a disciplined life of discipleship, we are preparing and being ready for those moments when suddenly we are called upon:

— to say no to temptation,

— to decide who speaks the truth,

— to recognize the presence of Jesus.

At those moments we are called upon to light our lamps and enter through the door that leads to the experience of celebration and joy. "Behold the bridegroom cometh." It can happen at any moment and it will happen at the end of our lives.

Following Jesus is building your life on a very sure foundation. It is a very wise thing to do. The decision is yours. Amen.

Is It Too Late?

To get his point across, a pastor once announced to his congregation: "Friends, I have some discouraging news. The building we have just completed is no longer ours to occupy. The bank is foreclosing our loan. We are being sued. It looks like we will lose everything. Beginning next month, we will not be allowed to worship in this building." The ears of the congregation perked up.

"The problem," the pastor said, "is that someone acted irresponsibly. The wrong figures were given to the lending agency. On the application for the loan, the figure of 2,000 members was used instead of 1,000. They claim we willfully deceived them and acted under false pretenses. The loan for the building has been withdrawn and the building will go up for sale next month. Perhaps it was wrong for us to trust our building committee to present the facts accurately. Maybe they were afraid we wouldn't get the loan if we were totally honest. They didn't do what we expected them to do. At any rate, someone acted irresponsibly, and now we all face the consequences."

This was, of course, just a make-believe story. There is a story just like it that is not make believe. This story has very similar dynamics and characters. It is the story told in our

69

text this morning, the story of talents and the care and use of those talents. This story can be seen as a story of another building committee, a story of entrusting to a few the responsibility to act with integrity on behalf of multitudes of people. It is a story of how serious the consequences are for the multitudes if the few fail to be good stewards of what has been entrusted to them. It is a story of trust, the misuse of that trust, the resulting anger on the part of the owner and ultimate consequences.

The property owner in this story is God. The building to be constructed and cared for is Mother Earth — the environment — the integrity of creation — all of God's beautiful creation. The building committee, entrusted with the task of creative use of resources, construction, care of and maintenance of this property, consists of you and me. We humans are placed in charge of this project. We are the building committee. God, the owner, has entrusted to us this property, just like it says in verse 14:

> For it will be as when a man going on a journey called
> his servants and entrusted to them his property.

The story goes back for its beginning — way back to the beginning of the biblical narrative in Genesis. "In the beginning God created the heavens and the earth . . . and God saw what had been created and said 'It is good.' " God placed humans in charge saying, take care of it. Keep it in proper balance so that it will work for everyone. Enjoy it.

"Let the earth bring forth its fruit in due season. Dress, till, keep the soil." The creator knew that the soil needs careful attention. God told those in charge to have dominion, tenderly care for, be responsible for the right order of relationships and resources. Then it will work for everyone's enjoyment. Be careful not to misuse it or neglect it. I'm putting you in charge. The elephants are not in charge, though they are bigger. The eagles are not in charge, though they see things from a better perspective. You, the ones I created in my image, you are in charge.

We are the building committee. We are the servants, the stewards of creation. We have been entrusted with the property. It is an awesome calling.

But my friends, we are being foreclosed on. We are being sued. We are in danger of losing our property. In a very short time, the doors will be locked. We will not be able to occupy the building. That which was made for us to use and enjoy will be closed to us. The doors are already closed to some of us.

Why?

Because the building committee, the human family, has not acted responsibly. We have not taken seriously the task given to us. There has been flagrant mismanagement. The facts have been construed or withheld for the benefit of a few. Resources have been abused. And now we all must pay the consequences. The day of accountability is upon us.

In our text the owner, the master, came to settle accounts with the servants, the stewards. It sounds rather harsh to read in the final verse. "Cast the servant into the outer darkness. There people will weep and gnash their teeth." How could a loving God do that? God takes care of creation very seriously.

Are we already experiencing the consequences for our failure to care for the earth? If we follow the scenario of the story, if the property entrusted to us is the integrity of creation, then it is not difficult to see that the outer darkness is the result of what's happening to the environment today. The question of survival and the possibility of an environmental catastrophe is just around the corner because someone has buried their talent. Someone did not act responsibly with that which was given to them.

About a week ago the headlines in the St. Paul *Pioneer Press* read "Ozone Thinning Quickly Over Us." The ozone layer, the wonderful protective shield high above us, that God created to protect us from some of the rays of the sun, is thinning three times faster than expected. If present trends continue, it will mean thousands of more deaths from cancer, say nothing of other complications. We, who live in the United States, with our chloro-fluorocarbons from air conditioners,

71

aerosol sprays and refrigeration, have contributed the most to this ozone crisis. But the effect of our action is spreading over the whole globe. We have discovered a large hole in the ozone shield over Antarctica. Many are asking: Is it too late?

Now add to that the global warming trend known as the greenhouse effect. We hear a variety of stories about this crisis, but everyone agrees on the fact that temperatures on the earth are six-tenths of a degree Celsius higher than 100 years ago, and it is rapidly increasing. The warming is much faster than predicted. There is disagreement on how fast we are warming up, but everyone agrees that it is a serious issue. We can no longer procrastinate in doing something about it. The biggest problem is the presence of carbon dioxide in the atmosphere which is produced by combustion of fossil fuel. This innocuous gas threatens our future on the planet earth. Most of this crisis centers around our demand for energy. Fossil fuels today provide about 80 percent of all our energy. The automobile is one of the main pollutants. In 1954 there were 52 million cars in the world. Today there are 350 million. By 2000 there will be 500 million. Once again, the industrial countries like the United States and Europe lead the way in the emission of these poisonous gases into the atmosphere; but the whole world suffers. Food production for the future could be in serious jeopardy. Many are asking: Is it too late?

Another sign that we are being foreclosed on and being locked out of our beautiful habitation is the degradation to the land, the loss of soil on the planet earth.

Cropland, forests and grasslands supply the bulk of our materials for industry, food and recreation. One third of the earth's surface is land. The rest is water. Of that one third which is land, only 11 percent is arable . . . usable to grow crops. Twenty-five percent is pasture and rangeland, 30 percent is forest — covered with trees, and 33 percent is wasteland, desert or paved over or built on.

Friends, we are losing ground. We are losing topsoil, that precious commodity that puts food on our table. The potential output from the land is being lowered because of air pollution and acid rain. The pressure for more food, more profits, more exports, has caused the loss of billions of tons of topsoil every year. The Soviet Union loses 1.5 billion tons of topsoil every year. The United States loses 5 billion tons of topsoil every year. Iowa at one time had 18 inches of rich topsoil. Today it has nine inches or less. Increased production of food that we get from the use of fertilizers, pesticides and irrigation are offset by soil erosion, water logging, salinization and air pollution. We are literally and figuratively losing ground. In addition, tropical deforestation is putting large amounts of carbon dioxide into the atmosphere and throwing systems out of balance all in the name of progress and profit.

Lester Brown, in the helpful resource called *State of the World 1990*, says that we are living in an illusion. On paper it looks like we have made progress. GNP (gross national product) is up. We are finding ways to produce more food. Most of us in the first world are better off than we were 10 years ago. But the world is worse off than it was 10 years ago, because the building committee is not acting responsibly. We are not getting accurate information on the full cost of our economic growth. Dean Freudenberger asks in his book, *Food For Tomorrow?*, if present trends continue, will there be food for tomorrow? Maybe not. Not if present trends continue.

We are slowly being cast into darkness while living under the illusion that we are prospering. We have buried our one talent. Soon we will wake up to the weeping and gnashing of teeth. In many parts of the world people are already weeping as is evident through the presence of hunger. Look into the eyes of the parents whose children die because there is no food. Environmental degradation is part of the cause.

Lester Brown gives an interesting statistic. The United States in 1990 spent 303 billion dollars on defense. The money was used for the creation of bombs, guns and missiles, to protect us from military threats. We spent in that same time 14 billion dollars to protect us from environmental degradation. That's a 22-to-1 ratio. We need to ask what good all our finest weapons will do for us if we continue to destroy the environment. A coalition of nations recently spent over 50 billion dollars, some say 100 billion, on a six-week war in the Middle East. A small country emerged as a threat to the source of oil and national autonomy. I wonder if we would be willing to wave our flags and blow our trumpets if we would decide to spend 50 billion dollars to prepare for and wage war on the threat to Mother Earth.

Is it too late? There is differing opinion on how serious the ozone crisis and warming trend really are. We all agree that is a problem. But how serious is it — 70 percent serious, 90 percent serious? Perhaps this example will help.

Your two-year-old is outside playing. Someone comes and reports that your child is headed for the freeway, exploring a new place to play. What would you do? Your child is 90 percent toward the freeway. You jolt out of your chair and head for the door. But someone else stops you and says, "Not to worry, your child is only 70 percent toward the freeway." Will it make much difference in what you do as a parent? Everyone who has studied the facts agrees. We are headed in the wrong direction. If we continue, we are in trouble concerning this beautiful creation God has given us to enjoy. Some may say 70 percent, others 90 percent, but the action called for is still the same. Stop the trend, or we will all weep and gnash our teeth.

What does the parable call for? Why did Jesus give us this story? What should we do as a building committee? By the way, building committees usually do a superb job. Ours certainly did. I use this illustration only to help us see how serious our responsibility for the earth really is.

What is our calling as stewards of creation? I will continue this sermon next Sunday. It is not too late. There are signs of hope around us. There are things we can do to change the situation. Remember, the reason Jesus gave this parable was to alert his listeners, not paralyze them or condemn them. Let me introduce for you today what we will talk about next Sunday.

What is needed first of all is an analysis of why we have gotten into this mess. We need to take a good look at our theology. Why has the church pictured nature as the enemy, material things as disdainful and economics as neutral? Has our theology led to the neglect of care of the earth? Are we so heavenly minded that we are no earthly good? It is a spiritual problem. The healing of creation needs to begin with confession and forgiveness.

We also need a better understanding of our close relationship to the earth. We are of the earth. God took dust, soil, and from it created humans. We need to discover what that means. Our connectedness to the earth needs to be reviewed, renewed and appreciated. We need to love the earth, remembering that God's redemption was for all creation, not just humans. The American Indians can help us in this area. Their spirituality keeps them connected to all creation.

Also, we need to restore and broaden the meaning of the concept of the steward. If we are entrusted with one talent called creation, then what does that mean? What is our responsibility? Can we redeem the word steward which has been used primarily to talk about money and financial campaigns? The story in our text is about stewardship. A steward is accountable to the property owner. So we need to talk about ownership and accountability. Will God forgive us? Will the third world forgive us? Will our grandchildren forgive us for failing to understand what being a steward is all about?

Also, next week we'll talk about the global implications of our lives as stewards of creation. How does what we do connect with our sisters and brothers around the globe? What does it mean to be a family, a global community? How do we love our neighbor 10,000 miles away whose survival is connected to our use or abuse of natural resources? How do the millions of cars we drive affect countries where almost no cars are used? As Jessica Matthews, who monitors global ecology, says, "We need a new sense of shared destiny."

And finally, what can we do to be better stewards? What can we do as individuals, as a community, as parents, as employees, as first world citizens? We will explore some options, some practical steps, some questions that we need to wrestle with. Next Sunday's sermon is an important part of today's sermon.

So don't lose heart. We only got started today.

Is it too late? Perhaps yes for some things, but not too late to reverse the trends and heal the land. We have been entrusted with some property, this planet, our habitation. That's like a talent. All of us are on the building committee. We are placed in charge of the project. We all want to hear the words: "Well done, good and faithful servant."

There is a wonderful promise in 2 Chronicles 7:14. It says: "If my people who are called by my name, will humble themselves, seek my face and pray, and turn from their wicked way; then will I hear from heaven and forgive their sins and heal their land." Let us look to heaven that God may forgive our sins and heal the land. Amen.

Is It Too Late? . . . Continued

Today we continue the sermon started last week. Our text is the familiar story of the talents in Matthew 25. We are concentrating on the care of the earth and its environment as an example of a talent — a responsibility — that God has given us. God has entrusted to us this property to care for. We are asking what it means to be a responsible steward of creation? And what are the consequences if we bury this talent?

When you listen to the tone of a person's voice you can often catch a feeling of how serious a situation is. However, when a person's words are put in print, you sometimes have to read between the lines to capture the tone, the feeling, the sense of urgency. Reading this parable in Matthew, one can sense the tone of seriousness and urgency as you read between the lines.

When I am called to the hospital to see a member who has been in an accident, I often ask how serious it is. The hospital has different words they use. They will say "The patient is in critical condition, or serious or stable condition." That will often dictate how quickly I need to get over to the hospital. As we listen to the professionals who are looking after the health of mother earth, the term they are using is critical — life threatening — urgent. If we don't respond with a sense of urgency, it may be too late.

77

That critical tone, that sense of urgency, is certainly found in the text before us. There is that element of judgment that catches our attention. "Cast the irresponsible servant into outer darkness where there is weeping and gnashing of teeth." That's God's word, not mine. I don't like it any more than you do.

God's judgment does not just come at the end of time. It happens all the time. There are present today elements of that outer darkness because of the irresponsible care of creation. Hunger and poverty are elements related to the abuse of nature's resources like water, soil and the air. It is not only preachers who talk of the consequences of poor management of the earth. Scientists and professionals in the area of ecology point to the same devastating suffering that is happening, and will continue to get worse if present trends continue. The question, "Is it too late?" is an appropriate question regarding the survival of the property God has entrusted to us. Is it too late for healing to happen? John Cobb, the process theologian from California, raises the ecology question in his book, *Is It Too Late?*

I want to continue last week's sermon by reminding us all that care of the earth is a *spiritual matter*. That is, it is connected to our inner being, our spirituality. It is part of our relationship with God. Our salvation, our sense of forgiveness, our joy and happiness, our responsible use of the talents given to us, are all connected. No one can read the parables in Matthew 25 and say that our stewardship is not a matter of salvation or our destiny. Read Matthew 25 while you wait for your turn to come up for communion today or when you have a free moment this coming week.

Some of us are still suffering from a by-product of an ancient Greek philosophy called gnosticism. Gnosticism said that mind or spirit is good, but matter and material things are evil. The body is evil. The soul is what's important. That teaching led to the idea that the way to salvation was through the mind or the spirit, and it doesn't really matter what we do about material things. Material things are not real. They are just shadows of reality. Such a brief description does not do justice to gnosticism. If you are interested, I suggest you read more about it.

The Bible does not endorse this negative view of the material world. "God saw everything God made and it was very good." Then God said, "Till and keep the land, manage it, tenderly care for it." That's the great commission in the beginning of the Bible. You don't have to wait until you get to Matthew 28 to read the great commission. If we are to take seriously the call to care for the earth, we must understand the spiritual nature of this call, its connection with our spirituality. Instead of pitting mind against matter, the spiritual against the material, we must see them both as important, as part of the whole.

Last week we talked about the nature of the crisis. We are moving in the direction of environmental degradation and catastrophe. The ozone shield is being depleted faster than predicted. The greenhouse effect caused by too much carbon dioxide in the air, is getting worse. The loss of topsoil is threatening food production for the nearly 6 billion people on this planet. The depletion and pollution of the water table are also signs pointing to future suffering. The present picture is not very encouraging. I think last Sunday we all longed for some word of hope. Is it too late?

One thing that gives us hope in the midst of all this doom and gloom is that it is being talked about today. It makes the headlines. Who made the decision that this article on the ozone shield should be the lead article? Praise the Lord that it did. (It's okay. Lutherans can say "Praise the Lord," too.) We ought to write and thank the editor. This is a sign that God's alarm clock is being heard. We are waking up. Maybe it's not too late.

Some industries and large corporations are doing things to reverse the trend of environmental destruction. I read the other day that since 1973 our economy has grown by one-third and during that same time we have cut energy use by two percent. Encouraging things are happening in the manufacturing and agriculture arenas, in government agencies. Certain countries around the globe are making important changes in the area of environmental protection. We should applaud them. Our critical watchfulness must continue and we must be careful to distinguish between cosmetic changes to quiet criticism, and changes that really make a difference. When we see changes happening, even the little changes, we need to affirm and appreciate. I am really encouraged to see how young people are becoming activists in their concern for the future of the created world. A friend of mine said his daughter won't let him turn the air conditioner on in their car anymore.

Here's another sign of hope. I've received several phone calls and comments this past week about my sermon last Sunday. Almost all were positive. Because people heard that I was going to continue the sermon next Sunday, some gave me ideas of things to say, things we can do. I was told by a professional in the environmental business that Minnesota leads the nation in dealing with solid waste. That's something to applaud.

One person I talked to asked me to be sure to emphasize the connectedness of everything we do. What we do with the environment has consequences — someplace else for someone else. For example, if you buy more paint than you need and dispose of it like other garbage, eventually that can get into the ground and cause harm somewhere else. You may not suffer, but someone else will. Half the pollution in the Great Lakes comes from pesticides sprayed on crops in Mississippi and Louisiana that blow up north. Everything touches everything. We are not just individuals whose lives are private and nobody else's business. What you do affects me. What I do affects your well being, and of course, this extends across the ocean, and it extends to future generations.

We all know the commandment: "Thou shalt not steal." That includes not stealing the future from our children. We may continue to put unsustainable demands on the soil which builds up our profit and provides cheap food, but it might be stealing from future generations. As stewards of the earth we cannot accept an isolationist stance. This applies to our individual practices as well as our national policies. To till and keep the garden, to be a good steward of the earth means being conscious of how we are connected to everyone. This earth is a home where we all as a family live together.

At some risk, I want to be specific and hopefully practical in suggesting things we can do in the care and use of this talent God has entrusted to us. You may have some other ideas that will work even better.

1. *Take Another Step.* I encourage you to take one more step in the direction of being a responsible steward of God's creation. Many of you have taken important steps — take one more step. If you have started to recycle, take the next step. Buy things that are made of recycled material. It doesn't do any good to recycle if there is no market out there for goods made of recycled material. Ask for — demand from the stores where you shop — products that use recycled material. You can buy recycled paper, recycled plastic, recycled tires. If you are shutting off lights not needed, take the next step; buy bulbs that use only a fraction of the energy existing bulbs do. If you have done things differently at home, see if there is something you could do or suggest at your place of work. Take one more step. Involve the whole family if they are agreeable. Instead of being paralyzed by the complexity of the problem, just take one more step that you know is needed. That's what stewardship is about.

2. *Encourage One Another.* If your relative or friend is riding the bicycle rather than driving the car, encourage them. If someone is hanging their clothes outside rather than using the energy of a clothes dryer, encourage them. We don't have to do what others are doing. We may not always agree. Maybe we haven't progressed as far as someone else, but we can encourage one another.

There are times when we may have to challenge, question and remind each other of things that we are doing that are environmentally questionable. That needs to be done in love. But the best way to help is by example, by demonstration. Someone in our justice support group decided not to get a snowblower that uses more fossil fuel. His driveway was not so big. Instead he invented a large, four-foot-wide wooden snow shovel that got the job done quicker than a snowblower . . . for most snowfalls. He didn't preach. He just demonstrated. Soon others were using that method and leaving their snowblowers in the garage.

A member of our parish whose heart is still back on the farm was talking to me the other day about how hard it is to convince some farmers to change their practices in farming. But he said you can demonstrate less harmful practices to the soil by doing it yourself. International development agencies like Lutheran World Relief or Church World Service have learned that the best way to bring about change in farming practices is to demonstrate, not criticize or preach or demand. We teach by example.

My point is, we need to encourage each other. When you see someone doing something to save the earth, thank them. In the long run we all will benefit. This week thank someone who is acting as a good steward of the creation, even though you may not be doing the same thing.

3. *Connect With The Earth.* That may mean taking time to notice the flowers or the birds or the change of seasons. My wife and I have this friendly debate going about my vegetable garden. She has the green thumb and has a beautiful flower garden. In recent years I've wanted to have a vegetable garden. She says, "Forget it. You don't care for it. You let the weeds take over." Then she reminds me that I could buy those vegetables for less than what I spend on my seeds, tools and fences.

Behind my reason for wanting to do vegetable gardening is to connect more with the earth. After all, my name George means "tiller of soil." I don't care if my carrots never make it to the state fair. I like the feeling of being connected to the earth.

Vivian's right, of course, in what she says. But so am I. Do you ever have those kinds of debates in your home where you don't agree and you both are right? Vivian agrees with me that it's good to connect with the earth, and we're both

82

working on that. I'm trying to remember to water the plant in my office and care for my vegetables as the season lingers on.

When my wife and I went to our tax consultant a few weeks ago, one of us commented on the large tree he had near the window. He proceeded to give us a half-hour lecture on trees. I kept looking at my watch because he told us when we came that he charges by the hour. I whispered to Viv as we left, "Don't ever ask him about his tree again. That lecture cost us several dollars." But I must say, he had a connectedness to God's creation. He loved his tree.

If you have some vacation time coming, may I suggest that you plan some time, some intentional efforts, to become more closely related with creation. Allow your soul, your inner being, to connect, to appreciate, to love, to become intimate with the work of God's hand. It could be a profound spiritual experience for you. It will make you a better steward.

4. *Become Informed.* There is a wonderful world out there that many of us are ignorant of. We can read about it. We can experience it. We can listen to the stories passed down to us from our wise elders. If we are to put a halt to the devastation taking place, we must get better informed. When you see an article in the paper about the environment, take time to read it. When you hear differing opinions, listen critically. Ask yourself who benefits from this approach. Who financed this research? Learn about the effects of our lifestyles on the third world. The servant with one talent went and hid it in the ground because of fear. That was a mistake. It is also a mistake to put our heads in the sand and deny the seriousness of the environmental crisis. We must continue to become more informed and more alert. It is a life and death situation.

5. *Accept The Economic Aspects.* Ecology and economics have a close relationship. They both have the same root meaning: the right ordering of relationships in the household. The trouble we are in is caused, to a large degree, by over consumption, the drive for more and more. So we have more and more waste and no place to put the waste. No one wants to store the toxic waste in their community, but few are willing

to consume less or stop the use of destructive chemicals. If we consume less, it will affect our economy which depends so heavily on growth. Much of the technology we have funded has produced economic growth, bigger yields, but it has cost the environment dearly. We must understand and accept the economic implications of caring for the earth. A good little book I recommend is called *Enough is Enough* by John Taylor. This book is very helpful in suggesting why and how we can be a part of the joyful revolutions that says enough is enough.

Next time you buy something, ask the question — Is it really necessary? Is there another way to meet that need or find the same happiness? Explore the ways to live more simply that others may simply live. Don't allow advertising to tell you what you need and when to purchase something. Ask not only what will this cost? Can I afford it? But also ask what it will cost the environment. Accept the economics of good stewardship.

6. *Accept The Political Aspects.* There are systemic changes that need to be made if we are to bring healing to the earth. Those changes involve politics. We become good stewards of creation by the way we vote, who we vote for, how we engage in the political process. You and I may do the little things like leave the lawn clippings on the lawn or compost it. It's not a big thing, but it is a move in the right direction. But if we only do that without a concern for the structures that are more concerned about profit than about the cost to the environment, we really are missing the boat. To save the earth we must all become more politically astute and active.

Before our state government at this time is the wetlands bill. We should be studying it. Let our elected officials know our concern and our support for responsible care of the earth. In two weeks we will have a letter-writing Sunday where we can all write letters to our elected leaders regarding the suffering taking place in the Horn of Africa. In the Food and Recovery Resolution for the Horn of Africa there is a concern for the soil in that part of the world. Letter writing is a political act. It involves a decision which is part of following the great commission God gave us when it says in Genesis "till and keep the soil." Little will happen to stop the trend toward environmental destruction until we take political action. To not get involved is to bury the talent God has given us.

7. *Pray For Healing.* We must pray for those who care for the earth and those who are destroying it. Our litanies, our songs and our prayers at worship need to reflect the concern we have for God's creation. During the war we all prayed that the wrongs being done in the Middle East might end. We prayed for peace. I hope we also pray for an end to the evil being done to God's beautiful creation around the world. Pray for healing. The answer to that prayer might mean a change in our attitude, our lifestyle of consumption, our decisions at work, or the choice of occupation. In praying for the earth, we should include a prayer for forgiveness for our neglect, our abuse, our cooperate guilt in the abuse going on. As we come to the altar this morning, let us come asking God to forgive us for the sins we have committed against the environment. God will forgive us. God's healing power is meant to reconnect us with the earth and energize us to be an instrument of healing and liberation for all of creation.

Finally, I am asking for a symbolic joint effort on the part of us all. Next Sunday, I am suggesting that we all come to worship by walking, riding our bikes or car pooling. Exhaust from cars is only one of our problems, but it is one. So let's do a symbolic gesture to help us all be mindful of our care of the earth. Get your bicycles ready or think about who you could car pool with. Get your walking legs in shape. We will call it Stewardship Sunday. Some may be surprised we're not asking for pledges.

On behalf of future generations, on behalf of people in other parts of the earth that feel the impact of our growing consumption, on behalf of mother earth, I want to thank you for all that you are doing to till and keep this land, this earth. May God, who created and established the earth to be a blessing for everyone, grant us to live in harmony with all of creation so that healing and wholeness may happen to the glory of God. It's late, but it's not too late. Praise the Lord! Amen.

When Will The Pain Go Away?

A young mother in her 30s with three children came to her pastor to talk about her husband's impending death. He was dying of cancer. "I'm afraid," she said. The pastor listened and asked a few questions to help her express her fear. One of the questions he asked was, "Are you afraid of losing your faith?" There was silence. "Yes," she said. And then there were more tears. There are times when one feels abandoned by God. If God really loved me would this be happening? Prayers don't seem to be answered. All those wonderful promises in the Bible aren't working. "Where are you God? I can't seem to connect." Doubts come into your mind. Maybe there isn't a God. You feel like Job's wife when she said to her husband, "Curse God and die."

When will the pain go away? How long can I hold on? Am I losing my faith? Where is God?

A friend of mine tells the story of how he experienced pain and wondered if it would go away. He is a seasoned farmer from Kansas who agreed to represent his church synod on a fact-finding trip to Central America. The purpose was to learn about hunger and poverty, and what churches in North America could do to help. He didn't think the trip was really necessary because he knew the answer. Farmers needed to

87

grow more wheat and be paid a fair price. Christians needed to give more money. More food and greater generosity were the answers.

The experience of talking to farmers in the Third World and being exposed to some of the root causes of hunger changed this Kansas wheat farmer's thinking. It wasn't a question of charity, he discovered. It was a matter of justice. The system needs to change or we will never really alleviate their suffering . . . and ours. The world economic order keeps the poor from ever getting out of the hole.

When he came back to share his story, he found a cold reception. He and his wife had lived in their community for nearly 60 years. They had all kinds of friends. But now it was different. People avoided them. It seemed as though they were inflicted with some sort of plague. No one argued or questioned what he shared. Their friends just didn't want to hear it. They weren't invited out to people's homes anymore. It was so different for them. It was painful.

The Kansas farmer had been warned that it wouldn't be easy to assimilate or articulate his experiences. But he didn't expect this kind of response from his friends and fellow Christians, those he had worshiped with for decades. He wondered if he had been duped and his hunches were all wrong. Could it be that he was brainwashed on the trip? Should he go back to the way he always thought? Should he forget about trying to help people understand why there is so much hunger and poverty? Life seemed to be so much easier before his conversion, his new world view.

Should I quit, he wondered. Should I go back to growing wheat, raising hogs, and stop asking the hard questions? If I do, would I be letting those people down, the people who asked me to go back and tell their story to my friends up north? I sure don't like this feeling of losing my friends. He wondered when the pain would go away.

Have you ever wondered when the pain would go away?

Your marriage just isn't working. The love you once had is gone. You feel like you have a housemate, but not a husband or wife. It hurts, and you are asking, shall I call it quits?

Your church has disappointed you. You have tried to promote more interest in helping others, in extended ministry. But everyone seems to be preoccupied with maintaining the church primarily for themselves. You've wondered if you should quit. You feel like you don't fit in the mainstream of the present direction the church is going. Will the feeling of frustration go away?

As a teenager you have tried to talk with your parents about your sexual feelings, but they seem afraid, too busy. You feel shut out. It is sometimes painful to be a teenager in today's world. Will the pain ever go away?

In our text Jesus tells his disciples that things are not going to be easy. "Beware," he says. Be ready for some difficult situations. Things may even get worse.

Some will try to lead you astray.

Nothing will seem to change things.

Killing and hatred will increase.

There will be times when you will be hated, let down, betrayed.

Things will appear hopeless.

Then comes this verse. "But the one who endures to the end will be saved."

To endure means to stand one's ground in the midst of difficult times. It means not giving up hope even though the outward signs seem hopeless and the pain doesn't let up.

All of us can remember times when we wondered if the pain would ever go away. We were tempted to quit, go back. Some of us may be in the middle of a difficult situation right now, and the question is, where can I find some sign of hope. I'd like to suggest some areas where we can look for signs of hope. First:

Embrace The Darkness

This is the opposite of denial. There are many wonderful lessons to be learned from "power of positive thinking" literature. Sometimes I think, however, it can border on a rather unhealthy denial of pain. Darkness and pain need to be embraced before healing can happen. It doesn't help to pretend there is no pain.

We embrace our pain when we give expression to our pain. Blind Bartimaeus called for Jesus to help. He cried out, "Jesus, Son of David, have mercy on me." Speaking out, giving speech to his need was the beginning of his healing. Things do not seem so hopeless when we are able to talk about our hurt. The crowd tried to silence him. Keepers of the status quo will always try to silence the cry of those who hurt, those who call for change.

We embrace the darkness when we stop running from it. Society is full of escape mechanisms. We want quick fixes. Take a pill if it hurts. Find a new partner if you are bored. Go on a trip to get away from it all. Have a drink. Sooner or later, however, we discover that avoiding the reality of pain is not the answer. Healing and wholeness happens when we are willing to take a long hard look at the reality instead of running.

Walter Brueggemann, an Old Testament scholar, talks about the capacity to grieve as part of embracing the darkness. He claims that our society has lost the capacity to grieve and, therefore, has failed to energize people with hope. Weeping, he says, comes before newness. Hope is discovered when there is a willingness to embrace the darkness. Jesus said to his disciples as he faced the cross, "My soul is exceedingly sorrowful . . . stay with me." That's embracing the darkness.

Be Rooted In Community

Hope is not a private virtue. It is not discovered by an individual effort alone. Rather, it is a gift of the Holy Spirit manifested in the gathered faithful. One of the main functions of the Christian community is to encourage one another. When things seem hopeless, we need the sense of belonging to a group that can be there when we need their support. It isn't so much in what they say, but it's their presence that sustains us. Our gathering together for worship each week builds hope in each of us.

Being in community can help us sift through the various options we have. Ideas will surface. Questions will help us look carefully at our analysis and choices. Sometimes we need to be corrected by the community where reality can be checked by more than one set of eyes.

Without the presence and experience of community, we can easily be led astray, act too quickly, fall into self pity, or feel worthless. When in the beginning God said, "It is not good that this creature I've made in my image should be alone" it was the clue for us to realize that we are made for community. Our decisions about whether and when we should quit will be easier when done in the context of living in community. Pain that is shared is easier to bear.

Hope is found when we give a high priority to sharing our lives with others and investing in a community where people care about each other. In Mexico I visited a small group gathering called a Base Christian Community. Weekly about eight to 12 people met in homes to sing, study the scriptures and discuss how they could act for greater justice. I was amazed at the strength they found by being rooted in community. There is no substitute for it.

Act In Love

Hope is the willingness to act before all the evidence is in. The author of Hebrews says, "Hope is the evidence of things unseen."

Hopelessness tends to paralyze us. When we don't know what to do, we may opt to do nothing. Sometimes that may be the better part of wisdom, but often we remain in the pit of despair until we act, even before we are 100 percent sure that it is the right thing to do. It is in doing the loving things that we discover the hope that makes life worth living.

91

My friend from Kansas could have crawled into a shell and said, "To heck with it. It's not worth the pain." He could have waited until he was more sure that everything he experienced was an accurate perception of the whole situation. Instead he prayed for wisdom and courage, but continued sharing his story. His action helped him sense a kind of solidarity with those who suffered and that kept hope alive for him. His pain took on meaning.

We seldom know all the facts. New information is always needed. One should never stop looking for more insight and knowledge. But our knowledge will always be imperfect. To act in love means to follow the hunches we have been given even before we are 100 percent sure. That's why faith, hope and love are always tied together. We do the loving things with the faith that God is with us and can forgive us if we are wrong. In the midst of this action we discover hope which in turn energizes us to hang in there.

Zacchaeus climbed up into a sycamore tree to see Jesus. He could have said, "It's hopeless. I'm too short. I'll never see him in this crowd." Instead he acted without the full assurance that it would bring worthwhile results . . . before all the the evidence was in. It paid off. He met Jesus and his life took on new dimensions.

Hope is kept alive when we are willing to take what information we have and act on it, do something about it, even before we have all the answers. In the doing we keep hope alive.

Learn From Creation

There are so many lessons of hope that can be learned from nature. Native Americans have taught us an important dimension to spirituality by the value they place on a close relationship to the earth and the environment. We would do well to reconnect with nature in order to sustain hope.

Those who live where the seasons are more marked and evident may have an advantage. But everywhere there are signs in creation of life coming out of death. Seeds are sown. They die before they spring forth to bear fruit. Babies are born from such a small beginning when a tiny little egg is fertilized by a seed so small the eyes cannot see it. Someone has said that every time a baby is born, it is a sign of hope, a sign that God hasn't given up on this world. God used a rainbow as a sign of hope for the descendants of Noah. There are many rainbows in nature that remind us of God's presence and promises.

Jesus used creation to build hope when he said, "Look at the birds of the air and consider the lilies of the field." Don't worry about tomorrow. God will be there to care for you. Instead, seek the kingdom and justice . . . .

Hope can be found in taking time to experience God in and through nature. Darkness happens, but after that the dawn. Look around and learn from creation.

Listen To Storytelling

One of the ways the people of faith in the early testament kept hope alive was in telling the stories of their ancestors. It became known as the oral tradition which served as the bedrock of their faith. If it weren't for storytelling, we wouldn't have much of a Bible. The stories of Abraham, Isaac, Jacob, Joseph and the Exodus were told over and over again to each other. They became sources of hope when things were not easy. God saw them through tough times. So God would not let others down in the time of crisis. Storytelling is a gift given to us, and we should use it to sustain and encourage one another. Again, the book of Hebrews is of help. In chapter 11, the author runs through a list of people of faith and briefly tells their story. Then chapter 12 begins, "Since we are surrounded by so great a cloud of witnesses, let us lay aside those weights and sins that beset us, and run with perseverance the race set before us." We are encouraged to persevere by the stories of the cloud of witnesses. Their stories build hope.

When I hear the story of Anne Frank who hid from the Nazis in Holland during World War II, I am encouraged. Hearing the stories of Steve Biko of South Africa and Oscar Romero of El Salvador always gives me new energy to go on in spite of resistance. They never gave up hope. Neither will I. I am inspired when I hear the story of my grandfather who came to this country from Norway by himself at the age of 12. Both parents had died. Relatives were too poor to care for him. He spoke no English. There was no one at the boat to meet him in New York City and no one at the train station in Lake Mills, Iowa. He walked the last 11 miles to a farm where a distant relative lived. That story reminds me that others have had it tough, too. It keeps hope alive.

Storytelling is often more powerful to keep hope alive than concepts, resolutions, doctrines, statistics or analyses. Stories resurrect the hope that was alive in those who have gone on before us. We feel surrounded by a cloud of witnesses. People of faith are a hopeful people because they are a storytelling people.

Hold On To The Promises

Hope is remembering that God is in charge. We are not God. Nor are we the Messiah, the Savior of the world. We may wish we could see things from God's perspective, but we can't. "Now we see through a glass darkly," the Apostle Paul says. Our knowledge is imperfect and we need to remember that in order to endure the uncertainties, the unanswered questions. What we have are the promises of God that have proven trustworthy and empowering. God's promises include:

— I will not allow you to be tested beyond your ability to endure.

— Blessed are you when people shall persecute you and say all manner of evil against you on my account. Rejoice — your reward is great.

— Don't grow weary in well doing for in due season you shall reap if you do not lose heart.

— Remember, I am with you always — even to the end of everything.

— Seek the kingdom first and God's justice — then all these things you need will be added unto you.

— When you have done it to the least of these you have done it unto me.

Hope is nourished and kept alive as we live in the promises of God. Not pious platitudes or empty ritual, but promises — promises from one who has been there before, one who goes with us on our journey, and who will be there to receive us when we arrive at the finish line.

When will the pain go away? I don't know. But I do know that hope is a gift of God given to those who embrace the darkness, act in love before all the evidence is in, root their lives in community, connect with creation, participate in storytelling and hold on to the promises of God. When we keep hope alive, we are able to endure to the end. Amen.

What's In The Final Exam?

When I was serving as Director of the Hunger Program for the former American Lutheran Church, I preached at various congregations on Sunday mornings. They would often ask me, "Should we read the Matthew 25 passage for the scripture lesson?" This text is a favorite for any gathering around hunger and poverty issues. I've used it often when I speak about hunger.

But the text has a far greater scope and purpose than to muster up a concern for hungry people. The story was not told by Jesus as a fund-raising speech. It was not intended for use in defending the need for a Social Action Committee, or the use of hunger funds for advocacy. One can use this text for many purposes, but we should not overlook the context and overall scope of its purpose as intended by the author.

This text takes us back to Genesis because it deals with the original purpose of God's creation, the ordering of right relationships and use of resources so that all creation may experience wholeness. It takes us back to the Old Testament covenant with God's people which included the expectation to do justice, love mercy and walk humbly with God. It takes us back to the beginning of Matthew's gospel when Matthew describes in the Sermon on the Mount what the kingdom is about, what righteousness is about.

Matthew writes to a church, not just a group of individuals. Some call it a house church. It was a household of Christians trying to live together and follow the way taught by Jesus. They were a prosperous people. It was most likely an urban setting and there was a strong Jewish influence. Matthew wants to remind them what Jesus taught, what was different and unique about Jesus and what this kingdom of Heaven was all about.

What Matthew does is to present Jesus to them and then he lays out some critical decisions they must make if they want to follow him. In doing so, he constantly reminds them of the resistance they will face, the same resistance the prophets faced, that Jesus faced. Matthew talks about the Christians' confrontation with false teachers, hypocrisy in leadership, and the economics of living in a household of people who claim to be disciples of Jesus.

Chapters 24 and 25 come at the end and are critical to this basic outline of what following Jesus means. Matthew has been leading up to it. He has been saying this and that about Jesus, about the kingdom, about discipleship. He had exhorted this house church to seek first this kingdom and its mission of justice, to enter the narrow gate, to love their neighbor and build their house on the rock. Now he reminds them, warns them in a kind of summary way, what all this means. Matthew is saying, let's look at the end in order to give meaning to the present. It is like a teacher telling the students at the beginning of the class what's going to be on the final exam so they can know what is really important to remember along the way. Matthew is telling us what kind of testing or evaluation will be in the finals.

I'd like to share four lessons I have learned from my reading and re-reading of this text in the context of the whole gospel.

1. *We are accountable.* It does make a difference how we live, how we respond to God's call. There will be a separation. Some will hear the words "Come, you who are blessed by my Father. Enter." Others will hear the words "Depart

from me." Jesus dares to draw a line between people. He sees black and white clearly. We tend to see various shades of gray. Nobody is a one and no one is a ten. Many of us comfort ourselves by claiming to be between four and six. We're middle of the roaders. Everyone does some good sometime. All of us have failed at certain points.

Jesus does not fall into that trap of relativity. We won't be able to hide behind our middle of the road theology. There are sheep and there are goats. There are wise bridesmaids and there are foolish bridesmaids. There is a wide gate and there is a narrow gate. Some build on sand, others build on a rock. There is God or there is mammon. You cannot serve both, Jesus says.

I'm glad I won't be the one who has to tell the sheep from the goats, and you won't either. What is important to remember is that we are accountable. There is a judgment. We will be asked to give an account of how we live our lives, how we use our resources, how we respond to God's will and purpose. In other words, Matthew is telling his readers, his students, there is a final exam in this class.

2. *The final exam is simple but not easy.* Throughout the gospel, Matthew has been talking about God's righteousness, which may be better translated as God's justice. "Blessed are those who hunger for justice." The church is to seek, strive for and participate in this justice. Jesus died to make this justice happen on earth. The kingdom of God, the reign of God is the fulfillment of this justice. Justice is the will of God which goes back to Genesis, to creation and to the covenant with Israel.

Matthew knows, as did Jesus, that we often make things complicated that are not complicated. So in this final section of Matthew's story of Jesus, a kind of let's get right down to the basics is the theme. What do we mean when we say justice — kingdom of God — loving your neighbor — following Jesus — having oil in your lamps — being responsible. If you want it put simply, here it is, says Jesus.

Giving food to the hungry.
Giving water to the thirsty.
Welcoming the stranger.
Clothing the naked.
Caring for the sick.
Visiting those in prison.

It's so simple it's almost an insult. And to add to the insult, the list is repeated four times in 10 verses just in case we miss the point. Where else in the Bible do you see something repeated four times in 10 verses?

Nowhere else in the sayings of Jesus do we find this detailed description of the last judgment. It is put very simply. You don't have to sift through volumes of theology or long chapters of introduction to get at the meaning of what the kingdom is about. It is so simple we can easily miss it.

What God wants from us is essential kindness, love of neighbor. What the righteousness, the justice of God is about is helping people who are in need. The church's mission is to reorder relationships and resources so that those on the bottom rung, the forgotten ones, are included in the blessings of creation. The kingdom is about people helping people. It is bringing healing and harmony where there is hurt and discord.

It is simple but not easy. It's not easy because there are many forces around us that make it difficult. Greed can make it difficult. Cultural and economic values can make it difficult. Structural systems and accepted traditions make it difficult. Misguided theology and false teaching make it difficult. Idols of worship and misdirected allegiances, ignorance, misinformation, lust for power, status and control make it difficult.

It may sound simple to feed hungry people, welcome strangers, and it is. But it is not easy. The fact is the rich are getting richer and the poor are getting poorer. Hunger in the world is worse today than it was 10 years ago. Tax laws continue to put a heavier burden on the poor. Women and children suffer the most from injustices. If it is so simple, why is it so difficult? The cross is a constant reminder that to love one's neighbor is not always easy or well received.

3. *There are surprises, unexpected discoveries, that disturb, yet serve to enlighten us.* Matthew includes these surprises now so that they can serve to warn us, alert us, help us not to be surprised when it's too late. Maybe the surprises are meant to teach us some basic theology.

Those who are invited to come and inherit the kingdom are surprised. Notice. "Lord, when did we do all those kindnesses to you?" They seemed unaware of the full implications of their lives centered around justice toward hurting people. Perhaps the biggest surprise is that the righteous don't claim to be righteous.

Likewise, the people excluded from the kingdom are surprised. "Lord, when did we not feed you?" You've got to be kidding. Everything we've done has been Christ-centered. We base everything on the Bible. Our pastors always preach Christ-centered sermons. Surprise! "I was hungry, but you did not feed me. Not everyone who says Lord, Lord will enter the kingdom of heaven."

Let's be honest. That's potentially very disturbing for most of us, not just the people in Matthew's church. What really counts before God is a list of things not often found on our list, our criteria for ultimate concerns. True spirituality is often measured in our commitment to Bible reading, prayer, church attendance, commitment to the church. All of these are important, but none of them are found in this final exam material. There is nothing said here about justification by faith, being born again, or baptized. There is no mention of belief systems, forgiveness, or proper understanding of grace. Again, important teachings in the Bible, but not in the list of criteria by which we ultimately answer to God. All of these other aspects of our theology are tested or sifted to see if they result in the simple goal of righteousness and justice. Put very surprisingly simple, it means meeting the basic needs of our neighbors, especially those who are victims of greed, injustice, and violence.

Another aspect of the surprise element may be the fact that Jesus claims to be found, to be present in the lives of the poor and oppressed. "In that you have done it to these, you have done it to me.'' It is a surprise to learn that by feeding the hungry, we are feeding Jesus. We serve God by serving those in need. It ought not surprise us because throughout the scriptures, God seems to side with the underside of society, those who have been left out, the voiceless and those who have been victims of oppression. When the Word became flesh Jesus was born of Mary who was among the poor of her day. The fact that this may surprise us could be an indication that we don't know our Bible very well or that we have interpreted our Bibles with a bias toward the privileged and powerful.

Don't be surprised, don't be disturbed when you are reminded that our response to the simple human needs of our neighbors — physical, material needs, as well as the need for love and participation in earth's resources — is what discipleship is about. If you want to find Jesus today, you will find him by feeding the hungry. If our lives are in tune with the biblical message, this should not surprise us.

4. My final point is on the *application of this story for the church today.* The reminder of being accountable, the simple meaning of discipleship and kingdom righteousness, the surprise element as a practical lesson for our theology; all these lessons can and should be applied to our ministry, our reason for being as a church. Matthew shared this story — given by Jesus — to help followers of Jesus focus on what is the essence of the kingdom of God. He wanted to show how the future coming of the kingdom impacts our lives today. This text, as much as any other, should be the guide for mission statements, budgets, programs and staffing in our churches.

I believe this story is leading us to *repent,* to *focus,* and to *celebrate* as we seek to reorder our relationships and resources in response to the good news of the gospel.

We need to repent of making complicated what is so simple. We need to repent of placing our primary emphasis on right formulas, right worship, right intellectualizing, rather than on serving human needs. We need to repent of our complicit acceptance of systems and traditions that have put people into situations of being hungry, poor, strangers, naked, sick and

102

imprisoned. We need to repent of structuring the church in such a way that it has been co-dependent on addiction to wealth and missed the essential element of mission. We need to repent of being selfish in displaying more concern for our salvation than for the needs of the least of these.

To feed the hungry today means more than simple food shared with those who can't afford bread. It means a change in the ordering of relationships and resources so that all people can share in the blessings of creation. For that to happen, there needs to be some radical conversions in the hearts of people as well as the economics of the household. When Matthew included this story of Jesus in his gospel, he wanted it to lead to basic change. God is calling for repentance. That is good news, especially for the victims.

This story of the great judgment is also meant to give us something on which to focus as we guide the ship called the church through rough waters. When you take another look at this list, repeated four times, you sense a central focus on people — on certain kinds of people. Their needs all touch the heart and call for a life of compassion. In other words, in all of our theology, our music, our worship, our programs and budgeting, there needs to be a focus on compassion and mercy for people, a focus outward.

This means that when we balance the inward journey and the outward journey in our spiritual lives, we will see the ultimate focus on our love for neighbor. The final exam will not be based on how well we did in silent reflection, improving our self image, being freed from guilt, but rather in how did all these worthwhile goals help us participate in righteousness and justice. A focus on the end always helps us keep our balance and make corrections when we go astray. Jesus tells us this story so that we will have a compass, a perspective, that will guide our decisions. We would be wise to come back again and again to this text to get refocused as individuals and as a church.

Finally, we apply this text to the household of God as we celebrate the grace of God. Listening to this story can be a grace experience.

— We celebrate the fact that we are given a peek at the final exam ahead of time so we can get ready. That's grace.

— We celebrate the forgiveness found when we fall short, when we repent of our sin of failure to focus on the least of these. We don't have to be tied up in guilt. We yet have time to confess our sins. God forgives. That's grace.

— We can celebrate all those who are today feeding the hungry, clothing the naked. They may not be part of our household, but someday the King will say to them, "Come . . . inherit." Instead of checking their labels or creeds, let's celebrate all who are involved in the ministry described in today's story. That's grace.

— We can celebrate the presence of Jesus we find today in shared bread. As we share bread at the altar, we celebrate his presence. As we share bread with the hungry, we know that he is present there. Let's celebrate those who have shared themselves with us. Jesus is present in the sacrament of bread and wine as well as the sacrament of people in need. That's grace.

— We can celebrate God's continual concern for this earth of ours, so beautifully created for all to enjoy. God hasn't given up. There is still a concerted effort to correct injustice, to reorder our relationships and resources. God's justice will prevail. It is this future hope that guides our present action. God's purpose in creation we celebrate. That's grace.

May God help us to re-read the story once more, the story of when it all ends, and by that re-reading, may God's spirit help us to repent, to focus and to celebrate. Thanks to our text today we know what will be in the final exam. Amen.

All Saints' Day
All Saints' Sunday
Matthew 5:1-12

How Does One Follow Jesus During The Threat Of War?

It has been difficult for me to decide what sermon I should preach today. I had planned to preach on the lectionary text in Acts which is assigned for this Sunday. That story of Peter and Cornelius has been occupying my thoughts for several days, and I had a pretty good idea of how the sermon would be developed. But the present historical crisis has been capturing the attention of us all. My sense of call as a pastor has urged me to set aside the sermon on Peter and Cornelius and speak about following Jesus in the face of the threat of war. It has come to my attention that I would be shirking my duty if I did not offer you some help in following Jesus during this critical moment in history. God's Word has something to say to us about war, about enemies, the use of power and the sword, and about reconciliation. It has a lot to say about peace. One of our beatitudes says "Blessed are the peacemakers for they shall be called children of God."

The Issue Is Following Jesus

My sermon is intended to help you follow Jesus. It is not intended to change your mind, your politics; or convince you to believe as I do about the real reasons for this conflict in the Middle East. Some of my interpretation of what is happening will surface in my comments, but you can sift through that without necessarily agreeing. What I don't want you to miss is the call to follow Jesus — not just believe in God — but follow Jesus. Following Jesus is what the call of the gospel is all about. My job as your pastor is to urge you to follow Jesus, which is a lifelong journey.

Following Jesus is not always easy . . . especially when it brings you face to face with ideas, allegiances, cultural norms and national trends that are in conflict with what Jesus taught and what he stood for. When we do things in the name of Jesus, we at times face strong opposition. Jesus knew that what he said would be a stumbling block to some. There is a "no" to the gospel as well as a "yes." Many of us have been struggling with how to respond to the threat of war, the possibility of our country's military involvement. The fact that we struggle at all may come from the desire within us to follow Jesus. How does one become a peacemaker when the talk is about war?

Following Jesus is not something that is done in a vacuum, in theory or in another world; it is not something that we can divorce from our daily lives, which includes our politics and our economics. Following Jesus is not something we take care of by going to church or sending our children to Sunday school and saying our prayers before we go to sleep. No, following Jesus is something that affects everything we do — our values, our work, our attitude toward sex, our use of money, and how we live as citizens of this world. Jesus did not give us the option of following him except in our politics or our economics.

Following Jesus is a lifelong journey. We continue to grow. We continue to change. We continue to understand more and more what Jesus and the kingdom of God is about. I was following Jesus 10 years ago, 20 years ago. But let me tell you, I have learned a lot in these 20 years. I don't think the same as I used to on many issues. Following Jesus has changed me. It hasn't come overnight. Don't be surprised if in this present historical situation you find you are thinking differently than

106

10 years ago. Following Jesus is a lifelong journey that takes you through many stages and growth experiences. Janet Hagberg and Robert Guelich have an interesting book called *The Critical Journey* which talks about stages of one's faith journey. I recommend it to you. If you are really upset with the way some of your friends are responding to the military build-up, it may be that they are at a different stage in their journey than you are.

In the threat of war or when your country is preparing for or thinking about war, how do you follow Jesus? What are your choices? That's the issue I want to address. There are moments in our lives when historical reality brings us face to face with critical decisions.

If you develop a terminal illness and learn that in one or two years you will die, you may ask the question, how do I follow Jesus in the face of a terminal illness? What are my choices? If you begin a new work and that work puts you face to face with tough decisions like, do I bend the rules to make more money, do I do as everyone else in the company to keep my job? How do I follow Jesus as a responsible employee of my company?

The same question must be addressed by us as citizens of the United States. How do I follow Jesus during the threat of war? It is not hypothetical. It is real. What does God's Word say to us about Iraq, Saddam Hussein, or about violence and killing Iraqi people? What does God's Word say about patriotism, about obedience to one's government, about following one's conscience? There is no simple answer.

The Scriptures Are A Resource

For most of us there is no chapter or verse you go to and say, "Okay, here is what the Bible says. That settles it. Either you believe it or you don't." There are no simple black and white options. We've done that with other issues haven't we? It doesn't work. We've done it with homosexual issues. We've done it with slavery, women's issues, the ordination of women, apartheid. Most of us, I hope, do not use the Bible to back up our bias or prejudice.

But there is guidance for us in the scriptures. I pray that the Holy Spirit may lead us to the truth and that the truth, centered in Jesus, may free us and energize us, may help us in the struggle. "God's Word is a lamp unto our feet, a light unto our path." "If we continue in God's word we will know the truth and the truth will make us free." This is a time to review the central message of the Bible. I want us to look at scripture to see how it can help us to follow Jesus — how we can be peacemakers.

Let me first address the argument for war found in the Old Testament. Didn't God's people go to war in obedience to God? War seems condoned in the Old Testament, it seems to be ordained of God. The whole idea of Holy War is found in the Old Testament. Doesn't God use war to punish, to bring judgment? Weren't the Israelites commanded to kill at certain times?

There are many things to be said about that. It is a difficult question, and a worthwhile question. Not everything in the Old Testament is helpful for ethics today. But what I want to emphasize is following Jesus. The Jewish rabbi from Nazareth, Jesus, seems to have believed that there is a better way to live than to kill and destroy, a better way to influence people, a better way to change the world. That is the way of love. "You have heard that it was said of old . . . but I say to you." He showed us the power of love. You can use the Old Testament as a justification for war, but I don't think you can use Jesus. Our concern is with following Jesus because we meet in the name of Jesus.

Let's look at a few texts. In Isaiah the second chapter, we are given the prophet's vision of what the coming of the Messiah would bring to Israel, to the world. It talks about God's visitation, God's action to save, God's intervention in this world. We believe — and here we may differ from our Jewish or Arab friends — that Jesus was that Messiah. Jesus was the new name for God, not the only name, but the new name. Something new was introduced by Jesus. Jesus came to show us the way to address separation, conflict, hate, greed; and so Isaiah talks about the Messiah way, the Jesus way, when he says: "They shall beat their swords into plowshares, their spears into pruning hooks."

If we were to use language that would be appropriate to our military weapons today, swords and spears would read: guns, tanks, missiles, nuclear weapons. God's coming to intervene would mean that nations, not just individuals, but nations would turn their weapons of killing each other into plowshares and pruning hooks, tools for growing food, for sustaining life. Weapons of destruction would be turned into tools for helping people live. That's what the coming of Jesus would bring about, a new vision, a new way of living together, of resolving conflict.

Isaiah goes on to say: "Neither shall they learn war anymore." I like that expression. Neither shall they learn war anymore.

War is something that people learn. It is a way of showing power to bring about submission from one's enemies. It is a way of solving differences of opinion. War seems inevitable when wealth or power is threatened or stolen. It's been around a long time. Perhaps we began "learning war" when we were given children's war toys, or when we watched movies and videos that exalted war. In the movie *Robin Hood,* there are more than 250 acts of violence. In the media these days there is talk of war. We are preparing, we are being programmed to think war, to justify war. We learn war when we gear our whole economic structure around war and the preparation for war.

Isaiah says that when the Messiah comes, when Jesus breaks into our lives, something radical happens. Our way of thinking changes. "Neither shall they learn war anymore." That's our vision and our vision shapes our thinking, our action. Following Jesus during the threat of war means going back to passages like this and reshaping our vision for this world.

Following Jesus doesn't mean just getting your sins forgiven and looking forward to heaven. It means seeking the kingdom and God's justice on earth as in heaven. It means living and working to bring the way of Jesus, his vision, into reality. That messianic vision was . . . "neither shall they learn war anymore."

Jesus' Way Was Different

Next I want to take you into the heart of Jesus' teaching found in the Sermon on the Mount. This sermon, we are told, is a collection of Jesus' main preaching. It's a kind of summary. If you want to get at the essence of what Jesus tried to get across, read the Sermon on the Mount. Here we have this familiar passage about how to find happiness and how to live as participants in the kingdom. Jesus points out that, in the Old Testament you read about an eye for an eye, but I want to show you a better way. He goes on to say, "Do not resist one who is evil with evil. Instead, respond with love." That's what turning the other cheek means. It means you use love, not revenge, as a weapon when relating to your enemy. The Old Testament may suggest that it's okay to hate your enemy, it's okay to kill. "But I say to you," says Jesus, "love your enemy." It seems to me that Jesus is suggesting that there is another way. One doesn't have to resort to killing and destroying. "Blessed are the peacemakers for they shall be called sons of God."

Now, many of us are very practical minded at this point, and we may say, it doesn't work with some people or with nations. That may be okay in the church or the home, but it isn't realistic in a world with people like Saddam Hussein or Noriega or Samoza or Hitler. This turning the other cheek just doesn't work.

But we meet in the name of Jesus. We may argue with Jesus. We may disagree with Jesus. We may disobey Jesus. We may choose not to follow Jesus. But don't change his teaching! Don't change his words to justify using violence to stop violence.

I want us to be honest in our struggle. How do you follow Jesus during the threat of war? Jesus said, "If you live by the sword, you will die by the sword." We can call Jesus a crazy liberal, a lunatic, or a wimp. We can choose to follow the empire instead of Jesus. But don't change the teachings of Jesus who came to teach us that love is more powerful than revenge, than the sword.

Perhaps the beatitudes give us the best clue as to how we follow Jesus, not only during the threat of war, but anytime.

"Blessed are the poor in spirit." Those who are able to keep their sanity and make good decisions are those who recognize their limitations as well as their potential. To be poor in spirit is like the first step in the 12-step program, which is to recognize one's powerlessness over one's addiction. It may be our addiction to wealth and privilege. It may be our addiction to racism or sexism. It may be our addiction to a war economy. The first step is to recognize one's addiction and seek help. Blessed are the poor in spirit, who sense their brokenness and need for help. This is not a time for rattling swords, but for soul searching and repentance. Is war the answer to our brokenness?

"Blessed are those who mourn." Those who find healing and wholeness are those who are willing to embrace the darkness in their lives. Often our tendency is to run, hide, cover up; deny our brokenness, our fears, our guilt. As Christians one gift we can offer each other is the gift of brokenness. "We all have sinned and come short of the glory of God." Sometimes our brokenness comes in the form of the pain of uncertainty, or the struggle of unanswered questions. We don't always know which direction to go or which decision to make. That can be painful. When war is the choice of one's country, maybe the first step in following Jesus is to own the darkness that comes upon us when we're not sure what to do. To mourn is to be in solidarity with those who suffer on both sides. Maybe this is a time for weeping as a sign of solidarity with all who will suffer if and when war breaks out.

111

We won't try to cover all the beatitudes this morning, only a couple more. "Blessed are those who hunger and thirst for righteousness, for justice." Following Jesus is to want more than anything the healing of people and society, the restoration of wholeness. It is called justice. This word comes from a first testament concept called mishpat. Mishpat is the reordering of relationships and resources so that all of creation can experience God's blessing. Jesus demonstrated that love is the most powerful instrument to bring that about. War seems to promote dominance and control. Reconciliation brings people together to share in the fruit of peace. Blessed are those who hunger and thirst for justice.

Finally, "blessed are the peacemakers." We all know that peace is more than the absence of conflict. Husband and wife may not be outwardly fighting, but that doesn't mean they are at peace. Law and order may bring an end to violence, but there may not be peace. Peace comes when all sides experience freedom to be whole, creative and participating in decisions that affect their destiny. Peacemaking is not obtaining my security at your expense. When I hear how people in the developing countries are suffering and will suffer even more because of the threat of war in the Middle East, I am reminded that peacemaking is far more than an end to conflict. One of the recent Popes said it well. "If you want peace, work for justice." As we seek to follow Jesus during this difficult time, we will look beyond the immediate moment, beyond the cost to us, beyond our need for security, beyond the talk of allied casualties. Our commitment to peacemaking makes us global citizens with a concern for all people. Following Jesus makes us members of the whole family of God. From that stance we make our decisions and take a stand.

I want you to know that it's okay if we don't agree on the issues that surround this crisis in the Middle East. I may be wrong in my analysis. At times like this we need to be patient with one another and forebearing toward one another in love. My prayer is that we may be attentive to the call to follow Jesus in all our decisions in life, especially in life and death issues.

Following Jesus during the threat of war may not be easy, but I'd rather be following him than to be following the way of an addictive society. It is a critical decision. Re-reading and reflecting on the beatitudes will be of help to each of us. Amen.

When Is Justification By Faith A Heresy?

Jesus was frequently dealing with people who needed correction, change, repentance, enlightenment or a new perspective. These people were often very religious, sometimes leaders of the synagogues who were well versed in the scriptures. They were people who believed in God, devout in their ways, and were eager to teach people the will of God as they had come to know it. They were intelligent and knowledgeable. But often they were wrong, misguided, blind or enslaved by tradition. Sometimes they had misunderstood the Torah or read only parts of it. Sometimes they had altered its original purpose to fit their self-centered purposes. Sometimes they had fallen into the trap of believing that blessing meant privilege, tradition meant truth, credentials meant insight. This led to arrogance and, at times, heresy.

I encourage you to read the gospels and notice how often you find Jesus correcting faulty beliefs or traditions. The scripture is full of stories of people who thought they had it all figured out but were wrong, or people who started out well but who didn't continue to be open to growth and discovery. When Jesus tried to correct these people or broaden their understanding, he often met resistance. Our text reads: "We are descendants of Abraham and have never been in bondage to anyone. What do you mean we will be made free?"

115

Those who said this to Jesus were people who had believed in him. They weren't outsiders who needed to be converted. They had taken step one. Jesus wants them to understand step 2 and step 3, as though to say, you're off to a good start but this is what discipleship is about. "If you continue in my Word." Discipleship is more than a start. It's a calling that continues. Real freedom means to continue in doing what the will of God is about. It is following Jesus, not just getting started.

Jesus wants them to know what the kingdom of God is about, what the bottom line is. A few Sundays ago we looked at the Isaiah 5 text and learned that the bottom line is about mishpat and zedekah, justice and righteousness. The kingdom of God is about the right ordering of relationships and resources among people and with creation. When all is said and done, what God is looking for is justice and righteousness. Last week we were reminded that the Great Judgment scene in Matthew 25 supports what Isaiah said. What really matters in the long run is how we respond to God's love by relating to our neighbor in need. "I was hungry and you fed me." That must have been what he meant when he said, "If you continue in my Word." Jesus was referring to justice and righteousness, the ordering of right relationships.

When this word comes home to us it may be as threatening as it was to the Jews in our text. We may be as defensive as they were because of our tradition, our self-assurance in what we have been taught to believe. There may be some things that need correcting — questioning — improvement — reforming in our church, in our ideas about God.

Let me say two things as background. Should you become disturbed or disappointed this morning, remember these two introductory words.

First, you don't have to agree with me. I may be wrong. God has not dictated to me what I am about to say. Everyone who listens to sermons should always ponder what is said. Test it out. Is it faithful to your understanding of God's Word? Is God speaking to you? You may not always agree or you may agree with some but not all. That's okay. We can disagree and still love one another.

Second, I want to make it perfectly clear that I am deeply grateful to the Lutheran Church. I am first of all a Christian, but I am also a Lutheran. The Lutheran Church has been good to me. I was born and raised in a devout Lutheran family. I was educated in the Lutheran system. It was my privilege to attend a Lutheran high school, a Lutheran college, a Lutheran Bible school, and a Lutheran seminary. I married a Lutheran and together we had Lutheran children. (ha). I have served four Lutheran churches and worked on the national staff of a Lutheran body. Through the Lutheran Church, I have learned that salvation is a gift and have heard the invitation to follow Jesus. I am grateful. I don't have any intention of leaving. There may be some things in the Lutheran Church I wish were different. No church is right on everything. The Lutheran Church is not above criticism or correction. I am glad that I feel free to say what I will say today. I say it out of love for my church.

It is Reformation Sunday. We remember what happened nearly 500 years ago. God raised up a priest by the name of Martin Luther who challenged the church to recover something he felt it had neglected or covered up. The church needed to reform, to wake up, to get back on track, to recover what it had lost. Both Catholics and Protestants honor the reformation as important to the life of the church. The reformation did not end when Luther died. The church is continually being reformed. Today, the Catholic Church, especially in Latin America, is challenging the church to remember its calling. Reformation continues.

One of the main teachings, if not the main one, that came out of Luther's theology was justification by faith. Lutherans believe strongly in justification by faith. Most Christians do. But this teaching is the prize and the pride of the reformation. No doubt the teaching of justification of faith is familiar to most of you.

117

Justification by faith means that we are accepted, and forgiven by God, not because we are good, or because we have earned it, but because God loves us. Our salvation is by grace alone. We are asked to believe it, receive it. Sinners are justified by "faith" not by works. This teaching is expressed in one of the hymns we sing; "Nothing in my hands I bring, simply to thy cross I cling." Justification by faith means you cannot earn your salvation. You cannot buy it. It is a gift. God initiates it. Christ died for it. God completes it. Salvation is a work of God.

I am thankful for that insight, that discovery, that teaching. It is thoroughly Biblical. I embrace it with all my heart. The giftedness of life and salvation, the gift of forgiveness and the promise of eternal life must never be forgotten or lost.

At the same time, I believe justification by faith has become a potential heresy in our church today. What do I mean by heresy? One definition of heresy is — a truth that is distorted, exaggerated, over emphasized; a truth that is not balanced with other truths. When I talk today about the heresy of justification by faith, I mean the use of it in such a way that it is distorted or causes us to neglect other truths, resulting in its becoming an escape from even more important truths.

Ernest Campbell, former pastor of Riverside Church in New York City, says that justification by faith is the most neglected and misunderstood teaching of the Christian faith. He says, "the term itself is heavy and the explanation usually given to interpret it heavier still." Campbell goes on to suggest that justification by faith is a starting point, not the goal of the Christian life. It has been proclaimed as an end in itself instead of as a means to the end.

I am wondering if the distortion of justification by faith has stifled the call to discipleship. As a result, we have churches full of people who have been baptized and confirmed but where few have taken up the cross to follow Jesus.

The primary focus of the Christian religion is the kingdom of God. Jesus came preaching the kingdom of God. His primary message was not justification by faith, but the kingdom of God. Everything else was a means to that end. His death on the cross was in order to bring the kingdom of God to this world. God is glorified when the kingdom comes. And so we pray "Thy kingdom come."

That kingdom or reign of God is a kingdom of justice and righteousness — mishpat and zedekah as learned from Isaiah 5. These two words mean the right ordering of relationships and resources so that all creation can experience wholeness. God blessed Israel so that Israel could be a blessing to the whole world. And what was God looking for? Justice and righteousness. "I looked for mishpat. I looked for zedekah (Isaiah 5:7)." In Amos 5, we learn that beautiful worship, right liturgies, music at its best, inspiring preaching are all regarded as worthless — useless when the people were not doing mishpat and zedekah. "Let justice and righteousness roll down like water." That's the bottom line for Israel and the church. That's what the kingdom is about. Being justified by faith is a beginning so that may happen.

When we move into the second testament and learn what Jesus' life was about, we catch the same vision. Did God change his mind when Jesus came? No! God didn't become more loving. Salvation was not easier. God's agenda for the world did not change. Jesus announced his mission at the beginning of his ministry. Look at Luke 4:18. Jesus came to preach good news to the poor and let the oppressed go free. Justice has always had a special focus on the poor . . . release of the captives . . . sight to the blind . . . liberty for the oppressed. Jesus announced a year of jubilee. That meant a new beginning for everyone. It was about justice and righteousness, about redistribution of wealth. All of Jesus' mission was addressed to mishpat and zedekah. It's there, clear and simple.

Everything we do and teach in the church needs to be examined by how it leads us to join God so that the kingdom might come. The work of mishpat and zedekah. That's what God's love is about. That's what the kingdom of God is about. That's what justification by faith is about.

It has been my experience that our strong emphasis on justification by faith has not resulted in a strong emphasis on justice and righteousness. In fact it may have done just the opposite. It may have served as an escape from doing justice and righteousness. Grace has become cheap grace and the vision of and energy for justice have been lost. Justification has become an end in itself. For some it has become a heresy.

I'll only mention a few examples of what I mean:

1. A distorted emphasis on justification by faith has led to an escape from concern for this world to an "other worldly" religion. We are so worried about getting ourselves to heaven — preparing for the next life — waiting for the final victory, that there is little energy or interest in working for justice and righteousness on earth. In church after church that I visited in my former job, I discovered that if they announced an adult forum on the second coming of Christ, the forum would be well attended. But if they announced an adult forum on Christian response to world hunger, only a few would show up.

We are more concerned about heaven than about loving our neighbor. That's a result of heresy in the church. Our hymnal is full of hymns about the next life and transcendent themes, but the theme of justice and peace is only found in a few. Thank God that's starting to change.

2. A distorted emphasis on justification by faith has resulted in a church that gathers people who believe in God but who are not following Jesus. We have pushed so hard to insist that our works will not save us, that there is little emphasis on the call to follow. Dietrich Bonhoeffer says it well in his book *Cost Of Discipleship*.

> We Lutherans have gathered like eagles round the carcass of cheap grace, and there we have drunk of the poison that has killed the life of following Christ . . . We have given away the Word and sacraments wholesale; we baptized, confirmed, and absolved a whole nation without asking awkward questions or insisting on strict conditions. Our humanitarian sentiment made us give

120

that which was holy to the scornful and unbelieving. We poured forth unending streams of grace. But the call to follow Jesus was hardly ever heard.

Jon Sabrino, a priest from El Salvador, calls for a new look at Christology. He says we need to recover the essential message of the gospels. Jesus said, "Come, follow me." When justification by faith takes precedence over the call to follow Jesus, we are in trouble.

3. A distorted emphasis on justification by faith has led to an individualistic, privatistic religion. Many people see salvation as primarily "me and Jesus," failing to realize that when you invite Jesus into your life, he never comes alone. He always brings your neighbor with him.

Nearly two thirds of church members are absent from worship every Sunday. Why? Many people today see the church as a place where we can slip in, slip out, without any commitment to the Christian community. After all, they are justified by their individual faith. My faith is between me and God, they say. I can worship God as well or better on the golf course. I don't need the church. That's heresy. I wonder if our use of justification by faith as a criterion to see if someone is truly gospel-centered is not partly to blame for this self-centeredness in our faith.

4. A distorted use of justification by faith has resulted in a kind of quietism regarding public life, an acceptance of the cultural values of society. There is little commitment to work for a more just society because the bottom line has been "getting my sins forgiven " — not justice and righteousness. There is a strong reluctance to take a prophetic stand against systems that cause injustice. We don't want to get involved in politics. We confuse capitalism or free enterprise with Christianity without asking; "Are we growing and becoming rich on the backs of the poor around the world?" The gospel is narrowly defined as our vertical relationship with God and the horizontal one is secondary.

121

In our churches there are symbols that help us in our worship. Many churches place the country's flag the same distance from the altar as the Christian flag, suggesting that we honor and worship the state and we honor and worship God on some kind of equal basis. That's heresy. I love my country but I don't worship the empire. The kingdom of God is about justice not patriotism. If justification by faith was understood to be a means to the end, the end being a world of justice and righteousness, we would not be as apt to divorce our politics and economics from our faith.

5. A distorted use of justification by faith has resulted in the absence of conversions in our churches. We Lutherans generally don't know how to talk about conversion . . . handle conversion . . . call for conversion . . . follow up on conversions. If someone comes and says "I want to become a Christian," we are likely to respond, "You've perhaps always been a Christian. You have been justified by faith."

The church is lacking in interest and involvement in mishpat and zedekah because many of us need to be converted to Jesus Christ, to following Jesus. We may need to be changed in our hearts. We may need to be born again. Something needs to happen on the inside of us so that the center of our attention is not our sins, or our getting to heaven, but the kingdom of God, justice and righteousness. We are weak in evangelism and the call to conversion because of our distorted use of justification by faith. Jim Wallis in his book, *Call to Conversion*, reminds us that understanding conversion, and the need for it, is really the central issue for today's churches.

6. A distorted use of justification by faith leads to an absence of speech on the teaching of judgment found in the scriptures. No one wants to be called a "hell fire" preacher. I certainly don't want that reputation. We don't want to send people home feeling guilty or upset or they may transfer to another church down the street. So we have leaned over backward to avoid the word of judgment. We don't talk about the weeping and gnashing of teeth like Jesus did.

Is not the cross about God's judgment, as well as God's grace? Frankly, the passage in Matthew 25 is awkward for us because of our strong emphasis on justification by faith. "Depart from me — for I was hungry and you did not feed me." Where is grace in that text? Did you notice last week how I skipped over verses 5 and 6 in Isaiah 5 where God removes the hedge and it does not rain any more on the vines. Verses 5 and 6 are a word of judgment. We are all eager to hear a word or promise, not judgment.

The scriptures, for example, say that to withhold the tithes from God is to rob God and robbing God brings judgment. We say, "give what you want and then ask God to forgive you. After all, we are justified by faith not by works." Does our teaching of justification by faith cause us to pass over the word of judgment?

What do we say to all this? Is there any good news? Yes, there is.

I want you to know we all fall short of justice and righteousness. I know I do. We need God's forgiveness. And God's grace is there for us. God will forgive us. Why? So that we might be cleansed and changed. So that we might join in the struggle for justice and righteousness, in the work of the kingdom. The good news is that God has not given up on us. The call to follow Jesus is still heard.

Jesus comes to us today as he came to the Jews who believed in him, and he says, "If you continue in my Word, then you are truly my disciples and you will know the truth and the truth will make you free."

We are justified by faith. That's God's business. Now we are called to continue in God's way by laying down our lives for others. That's our business. Amen.

Lectionary Preaching After Pentecost

Virtually all pastors who make use of the sermons in this book will find their worship life and planning shaped by one of two lectionary series. Most mainline Protestant denominations, along with clergy of the Roman Catholic Church, have now approved — either for provisional or official use — the three-year Common (Consensus) Lectionary. This family of denominations includes United Methodist, Presbyterian, United Church of Christ and Disciples of Christ.

Lutherans and Roman Catholics, while testing the Common Lectionary on a limited basis at present, follow their own three-year cycle of texts. While there are divergences between the Common and Lutheran/Roman Catholic systems, the gospel texts show striking parallels, with few text selections evidencing significant differences. Nearly all the gospel texts included in this book will, therefore, be applicable to worship and preaching planning for clergy following either lectionary.

A significant divergence does occur, however, in the method by which specific gospel texts are assigned to specific calendar days. The Common and Roman Catholic Lectionaries accomplish this by counting backwards from Christ the King (Last Sunday after Pentecost), discarding "extra" texts from the front of the list: Lutherans follow the opposite pattern, counting forward from The Holy Trinity, discarding "extra" texts at the end of the list.

The following index will aid the user of this book in matching the correct text to the correct Sunday during the Pentecost portion of the church year.

(Fixed dates do not pertain to Lutheran Lectionary)

Fixed Date Lectionaries *Common and Roman Catholic*	Lutheran Lectionary *Lutheran*
The Day of Pentecost	The Day of Pentecost
The Holy Trinity	The Holy Trinity
May 29-June 4 — Proper 4, Ordinary Time 9	Pentecost 2
June 5-11 — Proper 5, Ordinary Time 10	Pentecost 3
June 12-18 — Proper 6, Ordinary Time 11	Pentecost 4
June 19-25 — Proper 7, Ordinary Time 12	Pentecost 5
June 26-July 2 — Proper 8, Ordinary Time 13	Pentecost 6

125

July 3-9 — Proper 9, Ordinary Time 14	Pentecost 7
July 10-16 — Proper 10, Ordinary Time 15	Pentecost 8
July 17-23 — Proper 11, Ordinary Time 16	Pentecost 9
July 24-30 — Proper 12, Ordinary Time 17	Pentecost 10
July 31-Aug. 6 — Proper 13, Ordinary Time 18	Pentecost 11
Aug. 7-13 — Proper 14, Ordinary Time 19	Pentecost 12
Aug. 14-20 — Proper 15, Ordinary Time 20	Pentecost 13
Aug. 21-27 — Proper 16, Ordinary Time 21	Pentecost 14
Aug. 28-Sept. 3 — Proper 17, Ordinary Time 22	Pentecost 15
Sept. 4-10 — Proper 18, Ordinary Time 23	Pentecost 16
Sept. 11-17 — Proper 19, Ordinary Time 24	Pentecost 17
Sept. 18-24 — Proper 20, Ordinary Time 25	Pentecost 18
Sept. 25-Oct. 1 — Proper 21, Ordinary Time 26	Pentecost 19
Oct. 2-8 — Proper 22, Ordinary Time 27	Pentecost 20
Oct. 9-15 — Proper 23, Ordinary Time 28	Pentecost 21
Oct. 16-22 — Proper 24, Ordinary Time 29	Pentecost 22
Oct. 23-29 — Proper 25, Ordinary Time 30	Pentecost 23
Oct. 30-Nov. 5 — Proper 26, Ordinary Time 31	Pentecost 24
Nov. 6-12 — Proper 27, Ordinary Time 32	Pentecost 25
Nov. 13-19 — Proper 28, Ordinary Time 33	Pentecost 26 Pentecost 27
Nov. 20-26 — Christ the King	Christ the King

Reformation Day (or last Sunday in October) is October 31 (Common, Lutheran)

All Saints' Day (or first Sunday in November) is November 1 (Common, Lutheran, Roman Catholic)